ON COMPROMISE

ALSO BY RACHEL GREENWALD SMITH

Affect and American Literature in the Age of Neoliberalism

AS EDITOR

American Literature in Transition: 2000–2010
Neoliberalism and Contemporary Literary Culture

ON COMPROMISE

Art, Politics, and the Fate of an American Ideal

RACHEL GREENWALD SMITH

Graywolf Press

This publication is made possible, in part, by the voters of Minnesota through a Minnesota State Arts Board Operating Support grant, thanks to a legislative appropriation from the arts and cultural heritage fund. Significant support has also been provided by the National Endowment for the Arts, Target Foundation, the McKnight Foundation, the Lannan Foundation, the Amazon Literary Partnership, and other generous contributions from foundations, corporations, and individuals. To these organizations and individuals we offer our heartfelt thanks.

This is a work of creative nonfiction. The events, places, people, and conversations depicted here have been re-created from memory and some have been compressed, summarized, or otherwise altered.

Published by Graywolf Press
250 Third Avenue North, Suite 600
Minneapolis, Minnesota 55401

www.graywolfpress.org

Published in the United States of America

ISBN 978-1-64445-060-4

2 4 6 8 9 7 5 3 1
First Graywolf Printing, 2021

Library of Congress Control Number: 2020944179

Cover design: Carlos Esparza
Cover image: raindes

For Ted

the centre cannot hold

—W. B. YEATS (1919)

The center won't hold

—SLEATER-KINNEY (2019)

CONTENTS

IMAGES

ON COMPROMISE

1

CALL AND RESPONSE: AN INTRODUCTION

Show me what democracy looks like.

This is what democracy looks like, I reply to the call of the chant leader as hundreds of us march directly into a dead end. As we turn around and begin fighting our way against the crowd, which is surging toward the same sad fate, my friends and I discuss the obvious irony, that this is, unfortunately, exactly what democracy looks like: a passionate crowd stuck in a disoriented scrum.

We look for someone in charge. Finally, we find a lone shouter in a fluorescent green vest trying to make herself heard above the chants, waving her arms behind signs proclaiming the virtues of equality, her tiny voice barely audible even when we are right next to her. *One more block and turn right,* she says. And I can't help a thought that has nagged at me since I was a child. It is a shameful thought because it is a profoundly antidemocratic thought, one that verges on all of the things we are protesting: chauvinism, tyranny, authoritarianism.

The thought is this: *Why doesn't everyone just shut up and listen to the person in charge?*

The philosopher Jacques Rancière tells me that my hatred of democracy is ancient. "It is as old as democracy itself," he writes, going on to explain that the word was initially "used as an insult by those who saw in the unnameable government of the multitude the ruin of any legitimate order." My snarky interpretation of *this is what democracy looks like* draws from an older definition of the word *democracy* than the celebratory intentions of the chant itself.

Still I chant. Eventually, our group of confused citizens makes it to the main artery of the march. And as I chant, I mean both things at once. *This is what democracy looks like*: an incoherent mess of people who aren't listening, a crowd that can't see its own organizing principles, individuals who will not sacrifice their drive to get where they are going to an overarching plan. But also *this is what democracy looks like*: thousands of people demanding to be heard, thousands of people managing to keep one another safe without any clear direction. It looks like the possibility for collectivity, self-governance, and solidarity.

Because democracy refuses absolute authority, it requires a general acceptance of dissenting views, comfort with internal conflict, ad hoc alliances, and discouraging capitulations. And democracy requires compromises. Ugly, makeshift, disappointing compromises.

I am at the 2017 Women's March in Washington, DC, as a result of several such compromises. I have compromised on my skepticism toward large, permitted marches. I have compromised on my distrust of mainstream white feminism. I have compromised on my parenting, having left my kid at home for yet another weekend.

I have made these compromises, but I cannot satisfactorily account for them. When, two years later, in a class I am teaching about manifestos, a student presenting on the march's framing documents dismantles them in a convincing performance of intersectional analysis, I will have no justification for having been there, another middle-class white woman tumbling down the first knoll of middle age, shaking her fist at the impermeable edifices of governmental buildings and monuments. I will give the student an A, attesting on the evaluation sheet to a successful performance of everything I have taught: rigorous close analysis, a nuanced approach to contemporary pieties, a virtuosic performance of no-holds-barred critique. And I will feel conflicted, because I will recognize myself both in the compromiser, the person who went to the march despite all of its problems, and in the critic, the person who condemns such actions.

I am always finding myself in this trap, playing either the sellout or the hypocrite, the shill or the ideologue. All around me, I see vocal affirmations of one stance and strident disavowals of the other. You are either pathetically moderate or naively radical; an apologist or a purist.

Both of these positions, however, strike me as impossible to sustain. To take an absolute stance of refusal involves engaging in a Sisyphean process of self-purification, trying to scrub away the filth of complicity that will nevertheless continue to accrete simply from getting up and walking around in all of the rotten systems that undergird contemporary existence. As Alexis Shotwell writes in *Against Purity*, "We are compromised and we have made compromises. . . . There is no food we can eat, clothing we can buy, or energy we can use without deepening our ties to complex webs of suffering."

But to say yes to compromise, to believe, as Shotwell writes, that compromise will be how "we craft the worlds to come, whatever they might turn out to be," to say that because our current systems are rotten we simply need to learn to live, make peace, and innovate within them seems like the worst abdication of justice. I want to find a way of making compromises without celebrating them, to know the difference between compromise as a means and compromise as an end.

Compromises often seem either obviously good—as when intractable conflicts find a resolution because both parties agree to give something up in exchange for a solution that benefits everyone—or obviously bad, as in the accusation that one has compromised on one's values and is therefore ethically suspect, or disloyal. The philosopher Avishai Margalit places compromises in two categories. Most compromises, he argues, are political goods. But there are also rotten compromises, those that "establish or maintain a regime of cruelty and humiliation." This seems like a strong enough distinction, but accounting for specific cases predictably gives Margalit trouble. Was collaborating with the Stalinist regime in order to defeat Hitler ethically defensible? Were the slavery compromises in the US Constitution justified? Ultimately, he answers both of these in the affirmative. I find this unsatisfying, not because I disagree with his answers, though I might come to different conclusions, but because for me the very notion that compromises are either righteous or rotten involves seeing compromises as finished things that either shimmer or stink.

I am after the answers to other questions. Not what is the difference between a good compromise and a bad one, but how is it that despite the unsatisfying nature of most actual compromises, the eagerness to compromise has come to be seen by so many as a desirable character trait? How is it that the refusal to compromise is often cast as adolescent, obstructionist, or naive, while willingness to compromise is seen as a sign of maturity and trustworthiness? Why is compromise so readily seen as a moral good, even when so many compromises mean tacitly consenting to injustice?

These questions are interesting to me as a scholar and critic of contemporary literature and culture, because compromise has become a virtue in the arts too. Over the past thirty years or so, it has become more common for critics and scholars to praise compromise as an artistic approach, celebrating writers and artists who are neither doggedly traditional nor radically experimental. Artists have always brought disparate styles together in their work. But the widespread belief in the outdatedness of avant-gardism in the arts is something new.

In art and in politics alike, compromise has become not only a practice among other practices, but something to aspire to in its own right, along with other ways of avoiding ideological conflict: invocations of *you do you* and *do your own thing*, idealized notions of consensus, and simple acts of erasure—of conflict itself and of those who might provoke conflict. As a result, a begrudging acceptance of half wins and half losses has come to look like a political, ethical, aesthetic, and personal value.

That said, if you are reading this and thinking that your social media feed tells a different story, that the purists and not the compromisers are winning the day, then I ask you to read on, because these two realities are not as distant as they might seem. If it is possible to believe that compromise is a sign of virtue, it is also possible to believe that compromise is a sign of vice. Both positions stem from the same mistake: the tendency to confuse individual morality and choice with the structural conditions that are the fundamental material of politics.

On the day of the 2017 inauguration, I went on a long run through DC, mobs of young white men in red hats and heavily armed police vehicles dotting every block. I felt chased. Four miles in, I slipped on a patch of wet sidewalk and fell. It was drizzling, pitifully. As I lay on the sidewalk clutching my throbbing knee, the oversize numbers on my running watch informed me that the new president was being sworn into office. I held my breath. Nothing changed: same pain, same drizzle.

Soon, a group of college athletes offered me "a hand up" in a gesture of jock solidarity. I declined with as much cheerfulness as I could muster, too embarrassed for them to see me test my knee for fear it wouldn't support me. A few minutes later, an older man camped out under an awning nearby walked up and offered me a vanilla sandwich cookie. This, too, I turned down, putting on what I thought was a face of strength. He looked at me with grave concern. "You've been lying there for a while," he said. "I've been watching you from over there." He gestured at his sleeping bag. "Are you sure you don't want a cookie?"

"I'll get up soon," I promised, looking him in the eyes. His expression was familiar to me from my adolescence, a parental combination of concern, doubt, and tentative trust. He nodded. And as he walked away, I did manage to get up, trying out the knee, learning to trust it. Limping, then walking, then running again.

At the end of the run, I arrived at a food hall on the north side of town. Inside, I found women in pink "pussy" hats drinking wine and eating cheese at tables of ten, twelve, fifteen. Even though I know the truism that *the enemy of my enemy is my friend*, I felt lonely in that hall as I wandered from stall to stall in search of lunch. Maybe it was because of my dislike of those hats, which was inexplicably intense despite my love of uniforms, knitting, and cats. Maybe it was because everyone seemed so happy to be together inside, and I was preoccupied with what I knew was going on outside. Or maybe it was because when I lay on that damp sidewalk I had an intimation of what solidarity could feel like, even if it was fleeting, uncomfortable, and premised on the exposure of my vulnerability. But in a crowd of women who mostly shared my demographic categories (left-leaning, white, middle or upper-middle class, college educated), I finally felt inconspicuous. And knowingly disappearing into that pink-hatted mass felt like a compromise: unsettling and a little bit sad.

When I think about compromises, I think about that food hall. How it was not, in reality, homogenous. The food hall, if you bothered to look closely, was a space of potential conflict and of uneasy reconciliation. Yet the very thing that made the hall a place of relative peace despite that multiplicity also made it prone to erasing difference. My sadness was, in part, a response to how easy it was to give up my skepticism within that space, how convenient it felt to no longer have to negotiate my position in relation to that of others.

Compromises are containers for conflicts: they bring incompatible elements together into an internally contradictory agreement, practice, or action. Often this is a practical necessity, because compromises temporarily reconcile clashing positions when grappling with such explosive forces is impossible or dangerous. But compromises are also always in danger of obscuring the existence of the conflicts they contain by reducing them to what appears to be a single, comprehensible, rational answer. And it is from this transformation—from compromise as a provisional container to compromise as a singular answer—that confusion between compromise as a means and compromise as an end emerges.

This confusion may have been at the root of a puzzling set of survey results on the relationship between partisanship and compromise that was published by the Pew Research Center in 2014. Voters across the political spectrum were asked whether they preferred leaders who compromise or leaders who stick to their positions. According to the survey, 82 percent of voters on the left said they preferred leaders who compromise, as opposed to only 32 percent on the right. But the survey also shows that voicing a preference for compromise in general doesn't mean that one will support specific compromises in practice. In the same study, when asked directly how a conflict between then President Obama and congressional Republicans should be reconciled, the two sides equalized, with a minority—less than 40 percent—of both parties interested in making concessions.

What to make of the significant number of people on the left who attested to valuing compromise in principle but apparently rejected it in practice? One way to understand this discrepancy is to see compromise as having two distinct definitions. The first occurs when people disagree but want to move forward with something. This kind of compromise often involves feelings of resignation, as everyone involved knows they have given things up. The result is something no one can be proud of, but everyone has agreed to live with. A compromise, by this definition, is always singular—*a* compromise—something specific to a context, a moment in time. Those who make it often see it as temporary—a small step toward what they ultimately want.

The second is compromise as a principle or a general value. This is the definition of compromise that lies behind the categorical belief that good leaders are "ones who compromise." It is what is meant when people say things like *we need more compromise and less polarization* without saying what, exactly, we need to be willing to give up. This kind of compromise can be expressed not only through specific agreements with the opposite side, but also by a kind of bearing. A reasonable disposition. A tendency toward moderation. A suspicion of strong forms of argument or firm beliefs. This kind of compromise is more than a give-and-take. It is an affect, an attitude, a moral ideal.

When compromise becomes an ideal, it can be cast in almost utopian terms rather than being imagined to exist within the grim scene of most political compromises, in which both sides endure disappointment, accusations of selling out, and ideological crises of confidence. An ideal compromise can be imagined as beautiful; one made to be pleasing; a compromise that might be the end of the story, not the messy middle.

<><><>

In 2015, an anonymous antiracist literary collective calling itself the Mongrel Coalition Against Gringpo issued a critique of compromise in a satirical piece called "Gold Stars":

GOLD STAR FOR LOVING "HYBRID" BOOKS. BY HYBRID EVERYTHING THAT IS HODGEPODGE WHITEWASHED DISEMBODIED OH SO CLEVER HIGH FIVES FROM THE NYC POETRY FASHIONISTA CLIQUES

GOLD STAR FOR LOVING "HYBRID" BOOKS BUT MAINTAINING A NOT-SO-HYBRID CONSCIOUSNESS (ERASURE OF POETS OUTSIDE THE BLACK/WHITE BINARY, DELETION OF INDIGENEITY FOR THE UMPTEENTH TIME) . . .

GOLD STAR FOR YOUR DESIRE TO REACH COMPROMISE, TO SPLIT THE DIFFERENCE, REMAIN IN CHARGE: GOLD STAR FOR COMPROMISE!

The Mongrel Coalition's critique addresses a problem with how compromise is envisioned in literary culture, one that has echoes of similar problems in politics. Many works of literary fiction and poetry are stylistically hybrid. They bring disparate styles together into a single work, often aiming to reconcile the challenging experimental writing associated with the avant-garde with the accessibility of more traditional forms of literature. Many of the most critically celebrated works of the past few decades are hybrid works in this vein, from David Foster Wallace's *Infinite Jest* to Junot Díaz's *The Brief and Wonderous Life of Oscar Wao*; from Jennifer Egan's *A Visit from the Goon Squad* to the autofictional novels of Sheila Heti, Tao Lin, and Ben Lerner.

Like all compromises, these works can be interpreted in one of two ways: as vessels for tension or as evidence of a permanent peace. The Mongrel Coalition reminds us that hybridity can unmoor conventional social distinctions such as binary notions of race. But hybridity in contemporary literature often allows those already in power to "split the difference" and "remain in charge" by taking provocative experiments and embedding them in an easily consumable shape. I call this version of hybridity, the kind that aspires to use compromise as a solution rather than as a form of trouble, *compromise aesthetics*. And I think compromise aesthetics are ultimately bad for literary culture. Because if literature can be both digestible enough to be salable and formally interesting enough that readers aren't hungry for a truly oppositional avant-garde, the beneficiaries of that compromise are those with a stake in maintaining the cultural status quo.

Throughout the twentieth century, avant-garde movements aimed to disrupt calcified notions of what art is and how art institutions should function. But the notion of the avant-garde has fallen out of fashion in the age of compromise aesthetics, for some very good reasons. First, surviving economically as a writer is only getting harder, as the culture of work increasingly demands more productivity and more hours for lower wages, and as jobs in the arts and academia have become more scarce, competitive, and precarious. Supporting oneself through writing often means selling books and seeking well-paying readings at universities and other elite institutions. Embracing avant-gardism, which historically has involved adopting a position against art institutions, requires personal stores of wealth, hypocrisy, or both.

Second, even among the most politically committed artists, avant-gardism itself has become suspect. In her essay "The Delusions of Whiteness in the Avant-Garde," poet Cathy Park Hong documents how the definition of the avant-garde excludes writers of color despite the robust tradition of experimentalism among non-white writers as formally and historically various as Jean Toomer, Theresa Hak Kyung Cha, Ishmael Reed, and Karen Tei Yamashita. While this is undoubtedly a problem with the way the avant-garde has been traditionally understood, I agree with literary scholar Timothy Yu when he contends that many of "the communities formed by contemporary American writers of color can themselves best be understood in the terms we have developed for the analysis of the avant-garde." One need only look at the Black Arts movement of the 1960s to know that the avant-garde need not be imagined to be an exclusively white endeavor.

I still believe a concept of the avant-garde is useful today, even if hybridity is likely to remain the aesthetic mode of most contemporary literature for the foreseeable future. A robust concept of the avant-garde can help us see tension in aesthetic compromises: tension between the demands of the market and opposition to the status quo, tension between a desire to reach a large audience and a desire to disrupt expectations, and tension between the belief that art should appeal to a universal humankind and the belief that art can be a revolutionary weapon.

I see in art the capacity to provoke social change, and yet this book is, most emphatically, not a book about how art can save us from the polluted sphere of the political. On the contrary, it argues that we should look to art in this moment of political threat not because art stands outside of the corrupted world of politics, but because art, like we all do, stands within it. For me, this makes art even more urgent, even more relevant. We need to notice if our art is compromising in advance, if it is failing to provoke, to unmoor, to demand the impossible. Because if our art is making that mistake, it means that we likely are too.

<><><>

Once you start looking for it, compromise is everywhere. And there is a reason for this. Compromise is one of a cluster of values that is invoked in order to criticize the heightening of conflict, the cultivation of *us* and *them*. And this general impulse to eschew extremity in favor of moderation stems from one of the fundamental principles of American democracy: its commitment to liberalism.

Liberalism is a theory of political organization that values individual freedom, tolerance, incremental rather than revolutionary change, and the rational exchange of ideas. Despite the colloquial use of the term to refer to the political left, liberalism does not belong to the left or the right. As one of the foundational values of the American project (think *life, liberty, and the pursuit of happiness*), liberalism, in the United States, is more than a political concept among others. It informs basic assumptions about selfhood, teaching us to see ourselves as discrete, autonomous individuals. Compromise is a core liberal value because liberalism sees nuance as preferable to absolutes; negotiation as preferable to demands; flexibility as opposed to orthodoxy, and compromise facilitates these and other liberal principles.

It follows that challenges to compromise are often *illiberal*: they offer alternatives to liberal ways of thinking. I use the term *illiberalism* rather than *antiliberalism* because these alternatives aren't always explicitly critical of liberalism, particularly when they occur, as many of my examples do, in realms outside of formal politics. Avant-garde movements are often illiberal, as are subcultural expressions such as punk. But I also see illiberalism in some styles of art: in the oppositional structure of satire, for instance, or in rule-based formal constraints. Illiberal artistic and cultural expressions often experiment with the refusal to compromise, the insistence upon categorical rules, and the invocation of hard distinctions between friends and enemies.

Unfortunately, the most obvious contemporary examples of illiberalism in the United States today are associated with the far right. In an open letter published in *Harper's Magazine* in 2020, the signatories express the concern that the "forces of illiberalism are gaining strength throughout the world." Such forces, they argue "have a powerful ally in Donald Trump, who represents a real threat to democracy." These are very good reasons to approach critiques of liberalism with trepidation. Yet I do not agree with the signatories of the *Harper's Magazine* letter that illiberalism is essentially antidemocratic. It is true that fascism is inherently antiliberal: fascism prioritizes the myth of the unified nation over the rights of the individual. But critiques of liberalism are not only the domain of the right; socialism also challenges liberalism, and unlike fasicism, it does so in a manner that supports the democratic values of equality and popular sovereignty.

So despite the ongoing threat of the far right, I still think a measure of illiberal thinking is necessary today because of how destructive the liberal value of individual freedom has proved to be. In his essay "On the Jewish Question," Karl Marx argues that liberty is "the right of the *circumscribed* individual, withdrawn into himself." This circumscribed individual becomes the ideal subject of capitalism, which pits "*independent* and *egoistic*" individuals against one another. It is therefore not a coincidence that political liberalism, or the belief in the free individual, tends to come hand in hand with economic liberalism, or the belief in the free market.

Capitalism is only one of the exploitative systems that thrive under liberalism; racism is another, as is patriarchy. These systems, along with many others, connect and intersect, but they share some key properties. Because liberal systems are premised on the notion of freedom, they tend to disavow the violence they produce, attributing it to bad individuals who are acting immorally. This happens in relation to capitalism when the rich are labeled as "greedy" rather than as beneficiaries of a system that produces inequality. It also happens in relation to race and gender when injustice is attributed to racist or sexist individuals, leaving in place a structure that guarantees disparities on every level of society, from basic health services, to employment, to wages, to education, to housing.

Against individualistic moral explanations for injustice, illiberal positions foreground the social organization of power, seeing individuals as subject to the structures they inhabit. When illiberal perspectives place emphasis on power and structures rather than on individual choices and freedoms, compromises can be understood not as virtues nor as vices, but merely as the inevitable consequences of living in an unjust system.

My biggest concern about going to the Women's March was that it would be a weekend of being *nice*. Even though I am one of them, I associate being in groups of other white women with a feeling of paranoia; of always doing it wrong. And I feel that most keenly in the affect of niceness, a social bearing I have never properly mastered. Warmth? Sure. Affability? I think so. Niceness? Fail. Over and over again.

My worry intensified as I sat in the food hall among the pink-hatted masses. I was staying with a friend in DC in a house soon to be occupied by her girlfriend and several friends I had never met, stationed on pullout couches and air mattresses. I had arrived early, the only guest for the first night; by the time I returned to the house, the rest would be there. Despite my respect for my friend and her partner, I imagined the worst. I had visions of a happy puppy pile of guileless believers ready to smash patriarchy by means of Sarah McLachlan sing-alongs. I dreaded three days of smiling and nodding and trying not to say too much. I was certain that I would have to pretend, and that I would experience that pretending as a form of uncomfortable, stuttering erasure.

But I was wrong. As it turned out, the house was full of people who were not afraid of strong feelings, who were able to be honest even when honesty was hard. All of us, as it turned out, were skeptical of the march, but had felt driven to be there anyway. We talked late into the night over rye old-fashioneds, trying to figure out what we were doing there. We could come up with no rational explanation. But we had felt sick and scared for weeks. We were angry. We knew who our enemies were. And we were driven to protect one another.

I was, however, right about one thing. Once it got late and we were punchy with whiskey, there were a few sing-alongs to feminist anthems of the 1990s. But we chose Tori Amos, a songwriter who never sat right with most people, who wasn't cool enough to be reclaimed by '90s nostalgia, who was bad at being nice, who emoted too strongly, who was always too much.

Making friends is not political. And sing-alongs, like large permitted marches, are usually nothing more than emotional salves for structural afflictions. But staying in that house taught me something that nevertheless has bearing on politics: it taught me that compromise is only a shallow imitation of solidarity.

I think about my time in that house several weeks later, when I am back at home reading the political theorist Chantal Mouffe describing the precarious condition of democracy around the globe. Mouffe, unlike many theorists, does not believe that democracy requires measured debate or reasoned compromise. She thinks instead that passion and the conflict it can produce are good for democracy. "It is impossible to understand democratic politics," she writes, "without acknowledging 'passions' as the driving force in the political field." Making friends might not *itself* be political, I realize, but friendship might be an important engine of politics.

The passionate defense of one's friends in a democracy is a driver of polarization. And it has become a commonplace to say that polarization has put the US democracy in danger. But I think polarization is good for politics, good for democracy. Polarized people disagree. They argue. Sometimes they change their minds. Sometimes compromises are provisionally struck, but that doesn't mean that both parties necessarily come to the center. The disagreements continue, and sometimes power is disrupted, reallocated, or even undermined.

However, polarization, passion, friendships, all of these things are good for democracy, Mouffe tells us, only if they are driven toward political goals, focused on essentially political questions, which is to say aimed at the redistribution of power in a society. The problem is that thirty years of centrism, third-way politics, and technocratic utopianism have encouraged democratic subjects to believe that significant political change is impossible, and that to demand such change is naive or fanciful. The consequence of this, she argues, is that all of that passion has been directed not at politics, but at cultural distinctions, moral judgments, and empty partisanship. Rather than conflicting political goals, we have much more intractable distinctions: conflicting cultures, morality, and teams. Paradoxically, the culture of compromise has produced a situation in which compromises have become nearly impossible.

Many commentators have argued that both the left and the right have become concerned with purity rather than policy. On the left, there are demands for greater inclusion of members of underrepresented groups. On the right, there is the renewed visibility of white supremacy and arguments for cis, male, and heterosexual priority. These identity-based claims, the argument goes, are the basis for political partisanship, and they are what make partisanship so strong. Often the answer to this problem is the reinstitution of centrist policy makers who can make decisions based on reason, rationality, and instrumental logic.

Casting the situation this way is wrong because it equates the demands of the historically oppressed with the demands of the historically privileged, as if recognizing the struggle of people of color is the same as advocating white power. But more fundamentally, it is wrong to believe that political partisanship is the consequence of a focus on identity. Mouffe shows us the opposite: political partisanship and identitarian claims are more prone to essentialism when a focus on instrumental compromises empties the public sphere of the opportunity to engage in substantive political conflicts. And this depoliticization has led to a general situation in which politics is envisioned in moral terms, as a matter of right and wrong, of good people and bad people, rather than a matter of a negotiation over how power will be allocated in a society.

This book was written between the fall of 2016 and the summer of 2020. I will not know who wins the 2020 presidential election before these pages are finalized. I do know that the choice will be between a far-right illiberal Republican and a centrist liberal Democrat. The structure of this choice—fascism or compromise—has begun to repeat itself in political races in the United States and elsewhere: Trump versus Clinton, Le Pen versus Macron, Trump versus Biden. I do not look on either of these futures with optimism, even though I plan to vote for the centrist liberal, yet again, for the sake of the immediate impact on human lives and on the ecological health of the planet.

Today the questions that motivated my thinking when I began this project four years ago are becoming only more acute. The initial response to the coronavirus pandemic in the form of large-scale lockdown orders seems to eerily reflect my interest in uncompromising social policy, but in a form I never could have expected. At the same time, I see in the protests that erupted in the wake of the police murders of George Floyd, Breonna Taylor, and many others a refusal of the notion that structural disparities in power can be addressed with civility and incrementalism. I see in the scale of the protests, and in the fact that the mainstream left has largely moved to support them, a new commitment to democracy, one that has had to accept that democracy sometimes requires a rejection of liberal moderation. And this gives me a measure of hope.

I believe we are now late in the age of compromise. The foundation on which the center has stood—a foundation built on exploitation and inequity—is unstable. We see this instability in the volatility of the economy, in the decrease in US life expectancy, in the rise of social unrest, in the crumbling infrastructure, and in the weakness of so many of our social institutions. It is possible that this foundation can be patched, as it has been again and again, with compromises. But if centrism and compromise mean allowing resources to be drained from the many so they can accumulate at the feet of a few, the compromises required to maintain the status quo will get more strained, more based on a logic of scarcity, more painful for those who will get less and less from the bad deals they are being asked to make. Eventually, this foundation will collapse.

When I imagine a world beyond compromise, I imagine one in which the resources that are now being hoarded by the few will be available to the many. In that situation, compromises—the small, everyday give-and-take of living together—will be easier. Because it's easier to give something up in a situation of abundance than in a situation of scarcity. And because these compromises will not be made in the name of moderation and reasonableness; they will be made in the name of collectivity and solidarity. I know this world I imagine flies in the face of thousands of years of human violence and cruelty. But I still like to think that if we can just give up on compromise as a liberal value, we might finally be able engage in compromise as a democratic practice.

2

WELCOME TO THE JUNGLE

In my midtwenties, I played bass in a female-fronted postpunk band. The two guitarists were the songwriters, which meant that my job, along with the drummer's, was to mediate conflicts between them. One had a gooey sweet soprano and could write danceable anthems that she might have sold to any of the pop divas of the moment. The other sang with a husky-sexy alto moan from beneath her Chrissie Hynde bangs. Sometimes their styles jigsawed together just right, producing a song that was catchy and haunting, girly and tough. But sometimes their collaborations started out sounding incoherent: a monotone verse with an overwrought chorus; a sugary pop bridge to a refrain of staccato shouts.

In these situations, the drummer and I did what all rhythm sections do: We listened to both sides. We used our instruments to negotiate, drawing the divergent parts together with our arrangements. As a graduate student specializing in contemporary literary and cultural studies, I took on this role with particular enthusiasm. Writing bass lines was another form of textual interpretation. I listened carefully to the song, and, once I found the bits that struck me as the most important, I accentuated those moments through harmony, emphasis, or the most radical tribute I could pay to a particularly perfect guitar riff: the silence of my own instrument.

Ideally, bass lines smooth out possible frictions within a song. Listen to the bass in any pop song and you are likely to hear the bass player plunk through a scale to take you from the end of a chord progression back to the beginning. If it's done right, you won't notice this handholding consciously, but your body will register it. The listening will be easy; the melody legible. The song will feel like it just works.

But I didn't always do this. I liked to use my bass to exaggerate disjunctions, to create edges, conflicts. I played with a pick, all downstrokes, choppy and driving. My favorite distortion pedal was the Big Muff, an enormous metal box that turned the smooth tone of my Rickenbacker into a sustained, crunchy growl. I kept the volume on the pedal up. When I hit the switch, it amplified so wildly in our underground practice space that my bangs vibrated against my forehead.

I think my general desire to rough up our songs probably stemmed from my participation, as a teenager, in the Portland, Oregon, music scene of the early 1990s. An offshoot of the much more nationally visible scene happening at the same time in Seattle, Portland's music community emphasized opposition to the mainstream, rejecting all things marked as preppy, yuppie, or square. But despite this general ethos of nonconformity, the scene was characterized by a pretty stark collective stylistic unity. We wore ripped jeans. Stocking hats. Boots or Chuck Taylors. Tank tops or flannels. Maybe a V-neck sweater, but only if it was extra large with thumbholes worn through the cuffs. Maybe a baby-doll dress, but only if it was paired with black lipstick. Hair could be long, short, or dyed, but never clean and coiffed. There were *rules*. I wanted to impose a similar kind of oppositional style on our songs, something that said *this is us, not them*. I liked to make our songs meaner, putting rough sixteenth notes behind sweet vocal harmonies, adding a roar of distortion underneath a melody inspired by the smooth transitions of R&B.

In response, the songwriters would sometimes make an appeal for the integrity of *the song itself* against my desire for stylistic conspicuousness. They wanted me to play with my fingers, not a pick. They wanted me to be more versatile, more expansively skilled. *It's what the song wants*, they would argue. This rubbed me the wrong way, though at the time I couldn't really say why.

<><><>

It isn't ideological.

This is my partner's revelation during the first weeks of his MFA studies at the Iowa Writers' Workshop. *People tend to think of Iowa as a factory that produces poems that all sound the same, but that's not how it works,* he maintains. *We try to figure out what each individual poem wants and help it to do that thing better.*

We are living in a giant Victorian town house that seems to be falling down around us. The boiler issues terrifying explosions upon ignition. Cupboard doors drop from their hinges into our hands. On leave from my tenure-track teaching job, I spend mornings reading on the porch, while members of the fraternity across the street carefully position red Solo cups in five straight lines in their front yard.

What the poem wants. The song itself.

I haven't touched a bass for five years, but still, my eyelid begins to twitch.

It's not as if I don't recognize these claims as articulations of important intuitions that underpin the artistic process. I understand that it is a basic premise of most forms of artistic craft that artists should identify what is working at the core of their work and augment it, making it more visible, more itself. But this premise is not simply self-evident. It reflects a particular set of ideas about what art should do, and draws its power from the degree to which it seems like plain good sense.

After all, I think, one hand on my well-washed and blow-dried hair, the other on the hip of my Banana Republic dress, awash with nostalgia for my days of black lipstick and combat boots, *what was punk but the desire to make songs worse?*

<><><>

When we found out that my partner got into the workshop, we were driving west from our home in St. Louis on our way to the Ozarks for an early spring hike. His phone rang: an Iowa number.

I tried to focus on the road while I strained to hear the tinny voice on the other end of his call. The voice belonged to a well-known senior member of the faculty.

We believe that if we get the best people, we can make them better at what they do, he said. *We don't shape people into great writers; we discover talent and then we cultivate it.*

The spiel that faculty member gave during that first phone conversation, as it turned out, was more or less identical to a disclaimer that appears on the workshop's website:

> If one can "learn" to play the violin or to paint, one can "learn" to write, though no processes of externally induced training can ensure that one will do it well. Accordingly, the fact that the Workshop can claim as alumni nationally and internationally prominent poets, novelists, and short story writers is, we believe, more the result of what they brought here than of what they gained from us.

In his study of the rise of MFA programs in the postwar period, Mark McGurl uses this statement as an example of what he calls "a nervousness" on the part of these programs about their need to negotiate between two equally important beliefs about artistic creativity. On the one hand, artists are often imagined to be individual creative geniuses whose talents need to be left alone lest they become stifled by institutional shaping. On the other hand, the very existence of an MFA program makes sense only if one believes that there is something that an academic institution can teach someone about how to be an artist.

So which is it? Are artists natural-born creative individuals who need only to be encouraged to pursue their unique talents? Or are they made by institutions? McGurl's answer is that MFA programs are based on the premise that both of these things are true. They are institutions that produce creativity.

Put another way, MFA programs are not value-free, but the value they impose is one that, paradoxically, would seem to contradict the entire practice of imposing values in the first place. The value they impose is the primacy of the work: *do what the poem wants.*

McGurl has a name for this strange paradox. He calls it *systematic creativity.* Embodied, he explains, in "the proximity of 'creative' and 'program' in the term 'creative writing program,'" systematic creativity is evidence that institutions are not always standardizing, homogenizing, repressive organizations. Difference, diversity, individuality, uniqueness: all of these characteristics that seem anti-institutional can, in fact, be the products of institutions and other systems.

So the idea that one should do what the poem wants *is* ideological. Like any ideology, it's the product of a specific institutional context, in this case the MFA program. But the idea that the best writing comes from doing what the poem wants is a particularly difficult ideology to identify, critique, and resist.

This is, in part, because we are better at identifying ideologies that are repressive, those that tell us we must do something we don't want to do. We have a harder time talking about ideologies that are individualizing, those that tell us to be ourselves. And systematic creativity is all about learning to be yourself, about seeing your art as at its best when it is free from external influence. Except, of course, the influence of the institution that tells you that your work should be unique.

While the whole notion of systematic creativity might seem counterintuitive, especially when it is applied to art-making, which has, at least since the onset of modernism, been imagined to be something that acts *against* systematic institutional shaping, it is not restricted to the domain of art.

In politics there has long been a word for the kind of system that produces, encourages, and relies upon the expression of individuality: we call it *liberalism*.

Liberalism has historically been defined by the belief that individuals are free by nature, meaning that any imposition of values is a threat to that primary freedom. This belief reaches back to the work of John Locke, for whom humans are naturally in "a state of perfect freedom to order their actions." The purpose of governing, in this view, is facilitating the natural condition of humanity rather than imposing a particular set of beliefs.

Liberalism is so multivalent, so entangled with basic Enlightenment principles like individual autonomy and the primacy of reason, that any attempt to critique it head-on feels like a failure in advance. "The liberal tradition," writes scholar Amanda Anderson, "values the examined life in its many dimensions, including the rigorous scrutiny of principles, assumptions, and belief systems; the questioning of authority and tradition; the dedication to argument, debate, and deliberative processes of legitimation and justification; and the commitment to openness and transparency." Who could be against such things? One would have to be unwilling to entertain complexity, captivated by unnuanced ideological positions, rigid, unmoving, or unreasonable. Liberalism positions itself as the absence of dogma, the absence of authority, the absence of bias, the absence of prohibitory power.

Liberalism therefore seems to be a matter of subtraction, rather than addition: it's what's left behind if we get rid of power. Against this notion, Michel Foucault describes something that sounds very much like an MFA program when he argues that individual freedom is not a given. We have to learn to see ourselves as naturally free, he argues, and this comes from the shaping power of certain institutions and social structures.

"In the liberal regime," he writes, "freedom of behavior is entailed, called for, needed." Freedom, he argues, "has to be produced and organized."

From an early age, children raised in liberal societies are taught to be free. Education in these contexts involves encouraging students to do their own work and punishing them if they copy the work of others. In a liberal education, standing out as an exception is the way to gain recognition. Education in a society that does not espouse liberal values might look different. It might put focus on reproducing the arguments of others. On contributing to a group rather than excelling individually.

The difference between these two models is not the difference between natural freedom on the one hand and imposed constraint on the other. In both cases, patterns of behavior have to be learned and enforced.

So liberty is not, as most of us tend to think of it, simply a matter of releasing yourself from obligation. It is also the result of compulsion, shaping, force.

<><><>

On tour, driving on I-80 on the way to a show in East Lansing, Michigan, one of my bandmates put Guns N' Roses on the stereo.

In the middle of "Welcome to the Jungle" there's an amazing breakdown where the drums kick up and the guitars churn and then, just when you think the song is going to fall apart, Axl Rose's voice comes in, shrieking: *You know where you are? You're in the jungle, baby! You're gonna diiiiiiiiiiiiieeeeee!*

I screamed along happily. Envisioning myself, for a moment, as the leather-clad Rose, I let my voice fly on the high note. As if there were no limits on my expression. As if there were no question of the assertion of myself into the space. As if I had always been led to see my aggression as a powerful form of seduction.

My bandmates all looked at me as if I had just casually bent myself into a pretzel. They had discovered my unique talent. Now they just had to cultivate it.

<><><>

The dissemination of liberal values was an intentional aim of the founders of the major creative writing programs. In response to the rise of totalitarianism in the 1930s and '40s, the creative writing program was envisioned as a way of encouraging what was believed to be the antidote to authoritarianism: the individual.

As recent studies by scholars including McGurl, Eric Bennett, and Juliana Spahr have shown, creative writing programs were funded directly by entities such as the Rockefeller Foundation and even the CIA as a way of containing the Soviet threat. Creative writing programs were founded in part with the belief that there were political, as well as personal, reasons to see writing as individual, unique, and antithetical to prescriptive social positions.

The workshop turns out to be a great opportunity to teach the ultimate liberal lesson: *you do you.*

<><><>

Liberalism has been defined a dizzying number of times, from the seventeenth century to the present. As the principal system of belief underlying most modern democracies, it has also been practically enacted in a wide range of governmental systems, constitutions, and institutions. One value all liberalisms have in common, however, is individualism. At its core, John Gray tells us, liberalism prioritizes "the moral primacy of the person against the claims of any social collectivity."

When individualism is applied to people, you get *you do you*: the belief that people should seek liberation from social and collective structures that restrain their autonomy.

When individualism is applied to art, you get *the song itself, the poem itself*: the belief that aesthetic judgments are best made when they are not bogged down by a commitment to a given artistic movement or style. You get something that looks like the "Open Door" editorial mission of *Poetry* magazine, as articulated by its founder, Harriet Monroe, in 1912:

> The Open Door will be the policy of this magazine—may the great poet we are looking for never find it shut, or half-shut, against his ample genius! To this end the editors hope to keep free of entangling alliances with any single class or school. They desire to print the best English verse which is being written today, regardless of where, by whom, or under what theory of art it is written.

Free of entangling alliances, the editors are envisioned as appraisers of the value of each individual poem based on its own merits. This mission of editorial neutrality underpinned the magazine's image as a democratic alternative to the avant-garde "little magazines" of the 19-teens. And, perhaps as a result, unlike the brief interventions of most early-twentieth-century little magazines, *Poetry* has remained viable. More than a hundred years after Monroe penned her editorial statement, *Poetry* editor Don Share would describe his editorial practice in terms that sound nearly identical to Monroe's. When he is asked whether he prefers poems of any specific style or school, his answer is a clear *no*. "I think about whether or not a poem succeeds on its own terms," he explains.

Such an editorial policy allows for a great eclecticism of works, but paradoxically the very notion of being "free of entangling alliances" shuts out certain poetic gestures. The belief that each poem should be judged on its own merits requires believing that it is possible to tell the difference between a good poem and a bad poem, and that this distinction will not carry with it any of the marks of its context. But sometimes the entanglement is the point—as it is with art that is important because of its alliance with a specific aesthetic movement, or art that is important because of its engagement with a specific political cause or context. And sometimes alliances are the strongest where they are most disavowed. The archive of *Poetry* suggests that the Open Door policy is tautological. The magazine, a vehicle for prestige, has published the most prestigious poets of the twentieth and twenty-first centuries. Free of entangling alliances, free to publish only the best, the magazine is allied with a model of art that rests on a belief in meritocracy, individualism, and excellence as a decontextualized feature of individual works of art.

<><><>

When I was a Guns N' Roses fan, my other favorite bands sprawled across genres. From Nine Inch Nails to Pearl Jam, from the Dead Kennedys to L7, from the Legendary Pink Dots to the Specials, I liked it all: industrial, punk, goth, ska, anything that was staged as a hostile response to what surrounded me as the norm, which was the '80s pop sensibility that lingered into the early '90s, as Bryan Adams and Amy Grant crooned out Hot 100 hits well into 1991.

It wasn't the pop songs themselves that I hated. (I still secretly listened to C+C Music Factory, Paula Abdul, and Boyz II Men on my Walkman, the transparent window facing toward my hip.) I hated the straight-haired blond girls whose signature scent—Fuzzy Peach perfume from the Body Shop—drenched not only the middle school's hallways but also any space where those songs were played: the gym during dances, the mall, the back of the school bus. But it didn't take me long to realize that there was a difference between Guns N' Roses and the bands I later came to love, and it wasn't just about ten-minute-long-guitar-solos versus three-chords-and-the-truth.

Guns N' Roses cultivated a scene marked by conventional gender norms. Their lyrics were explicitly hateful toward women and gay men. Axl was an incredible front man, but he achieved his magnetism by thrusting himself aggressively onto his audience in such a way that always suggested the possibility of masculine violence.

FUCK you. SUCK my FUCKING DICK, he proclaimed, proudly, in "Get in the Ring," once one of my favorite songs. I loved yelling along with it, for a while. But then I realized that it mattered that those words weren't written for my mouth.

Instead, the community I came to love was one in which your participation in the scene counted in terms of how your work was received. If you shared your practice space, if you told the bros in the pit to move to the back so that girls could see and not be trampled, if you told people to buy the tape of the opening band rather than your own, if you sat in on backing vocals and invited others to do the same for you, people would go to your shows and buy your stuff, even if your band was just okay.

There were still problems, of course. The bands were still primarily, though not exclusively, white and male. The scene had its own hierarchies, its own exclusions. And while some of these, such as the general prohibition of macho displays of strength and bravado, made the spaces of shows and record stores feel safer to me, others, such as the broad tendency for women to be band managers, booking agents, girlfriends, and merch sellers rather than musicians, left me hungry for other possibilities.

But despite all of this and despite my being too young and shy to be integral to the scene, simply listening to music associated with that community, going to shows, and hanging out in local record stores gave me a sense that the whole world wasn't organized according to a logic of craven competition, violence, money, and celebrity.

I go back and listen to some of my favorite records from that time, records by Pond, Hazel, the Spinanes, Thirty Ought Six, and Quasi, the cardboard corners of their sleeves worn and soft, the sound of the vinyl mushy under the dusty needle of my record player. Some of them, like Quasi's *R&B Transmogrification*, are truly incredible recordings that just never circulated beyond a small group of local fans. But when I try out listening to them as I imagine someone with no knowledge of their context might hear them—as individual songs to be measured according to their own merits—I'm astonished at how technically bad some of my very favorites are. I listen to Hazel's *Toreador of Love* and am struck by how the tempo sometimes drags and sometimes races, how off-key Pete Krebs's and Jodi Bleyle's harmonies are. And yet, I still love the songs. I love them because the particular ways in which they are bad signal their membership in an aesthetic movement. Their tempos are inconsistent because they would never have dreamed of recording to a metronome click, as I did, diligently, on our band's first EP. The harmonies are off-key in a way that highlights the distance between Krebs's and Bleyle's voices, making the record more about the experiment of bringing two radically different musicians together than showcasing their technical prowess. And that particular blend of off-key, tempo-dragging badness still makes me feel like a part of something specific, something that wasn't governed by the social and aesthetic norms of the moment.

If Guns N' Roses made technically good music that was actually bad, a lot of these songs were technically bad songs that were really, really good, because technical proficiency wasn't what mattered. What mattered was living with and for a collective sense of belonging. And if that could be heard in the songs themselves, it was in the way they sounded the same as much as it was in what made them unique.

<><><>

New York in the 2000s was not Portland in the 1990s. My band booked shows by the time slot rather than by the bill, which meant that on a given night at the Mercury Lounge, you could have five different bands of five different genres playing one after the other. This benefited the club, because it meant that they got five different crowds coming in and out on a single night. In theory, they could quintuple what they made from cover charges.

When you gave your ten bucks to the doorman, he would put a little hash mark by the name of the band you said you were there to see. And, at the end of the night, the bands with a lot of hash marks got asked back. The ones with fewer would have to go elsewhere for their next show. Bookers also scanned the room during each band's set, informally counting bodies and roughly tabulating drink sales.

When we played live, we were aware that the fact of our gender was our greatest draw, a strange paradox because our gender was also the thing that made daily aspects of our work harder. It was hard to get strings, because it was nearly impossible to get the exclusively male employees at guitar stores to see us as anything but lost girlfriends wandering aimlessly. And once we did manage to get their attention, the problems got worse. Guitar store employees tried to convince me that I wanted light gauge strings because medium gauge would be too hard for my fingers to press down. They refused to set up my bass as I wanted it because they worried that the action that would give me the tone I wanted would make it too hard for me to play. Sound check was another ordeal, where the working assumption seemed to be that we didn't know how our amps worked, that we needed men to tell us how to plug in and how to set up our pedals.

But crowds loved seeing women play electric guitars, so we would storm the stage the moment the band before us unplugged, hoping the audience could see us in our tight jeans and maybe decide to stay for the first song. Looking sultry while we were tuning became part of our schtick. I would grit my teeth and do my best to flirt with any guy who approached me between sets, no matter how creepy or boring he seemed, because his was a body in the room that might be counted.

The entire New York music scene resembled a giant reality television show. Would you get cut or brought back for another shot? It all depended on whether you could outdraw the band that played before or after you. Bookers didn't see themselves as conveners of a community. They weren't looking for stylistic unity, but they weren't particularly attuned to the quality of the songs themselves either. They were simply looking for a salable product. And that meant that the more you could stand out, the more likely it was that you could move up the ladder of time slots and venues. Even though I was pretty sure that the fact that we were women meant that our songs would never be listened to as the songs themselves, our gender made us a novelty, and, in the marketplace of New York venue booking, that helped us compete.

Something similar happened at *Poetry* magazine. The magazine's Open Door editorial policy ensured that it held, for many decades, a relatively innocuous place in literary culture with a steady circulation of twelve thousand copies or so. Publishing in *Poetry* was a sign of prestige, but the magazine had a reputation for conservatism, publishing poets who had already been widely recognized and supported by other literary institutions.

But then in 2002, Ruth Lilly, heir to the Eli Lilly pharmaceutical fortune, announced a bequest valued at over $100 million to the magazine. John Barr, a poet and Wall Street businessman with a Harvard MBA, was brought on as president of what became the Poetry Foundation.

In an essay published in the magazine soon after the gift, Barr discusses the editorial orientation of the magazine in economic terms. "Predicting the future path of poetry," he writes, "is like trying to predict the stock market." Nevertheless, he expresses certainty that poetry needs to move away from the academy and toward "a general, interested public."

Presumably drawing on his career in finance, he suggests that the magazine could profit by taking more risks. "The human mind is a marketplace," Barr writes. And in order to compete in this marketplace, poetry has to meet "a standard of pleasure as well as profundity."

Poetry began to pursue that market. Its entrepreneurial spirit blossomed, first under the editorial leadership of Christian Wiman, who was followed, in 2013, by Don Share. Wiman writes that when he became editor "not enough young poets were sending their work" to Poetry. "It was just sleepy," he explains. "I tried to put something in every issue that would be provocative in some way." He also brought on younger writers "with sharp opinions . . . and some flair." Poetry began to publish work with a more experimental edge. It championed work by writers in translation, writers of color, queer writers, trans writers, and writers without institutional support. The style of the magazine changed: eclecticism and pluralism replaced quietism.

I began to find myself reading issues of Poetry left lying around the house, surprised at how many writers I admired were represented in its pages. There were poems that were weirder or more challenging than I expected to see in the magazine, like the typographical experiments of Douglas Kearney. And there were poets who had been writing for over four decades, like Mei-mei Berssenbrugge, whose work would have registered as too difficult or unconventional for the magazine a decade earlier. There were special issues that showcased the work of writers in context. And, as time passed, a new Poetry canon began to emerge, one that was younger, less white, less male, and less aesthetically traditional. Their names soon began to appear not only in Poetry, but in other publications, too, as prestige begets prestige. It was a relief to see the ubiquity of Billy Collins replaced by Ocean Vuong. Poetry seemed to be the vehicle for a substantive shift in the culture of poetry at large, a surprising role for a magazine that had once seemed so risk averse. And I must not have been the only one who started reading *Poetry* with more interest. The strategy as a whole paid off. Circulation more than doubled.

What I didn't know at the time was that while the poems and poets published in *Poetry* made the magazine seem more democratic, the Ruth Lilly gift meant that the material reality of the institution was becoming more, rather than less, focused on fostering individual prestige. I learned this only when an open letter addressed to the Poetry Foundation leadership was circulated during the wave of protests that followed the murder of George Floyd. The letter argued that the Poetry Foundation was guilty of hoarding its resources and using its promotion of some poets of color as a screen for the overall whiteness of the institution. *Poetry* may have looked like a vehicle for pluralism, but its institutional culture was still what it always had been: white, male, and rich. The letter was written by a number of the poets I had admired in the magazine's pages—Vuong, as well as Kaveh Akbar, Danez Smith, Wendy Xu, and others—and it was signed by more than fifteen hundred others.

But although I learned of the institution's structural problems from that first letter, its arguments didn't surprise me. The problems its authors observed were serious, but they were problems that nearly all lavishly funded foundations face. A second letter, however, really struck me and got me thinking about how liberalism makes itself felt in the arts today.

That second letter was written by poet Phillip B. Williams, a former Poetry Foundation Ruth Lilly Fellow. In the letter, Williams explains that he could not sign on to the original open letter, because he felt that it did not sufficiently foreground the complicity of people like himself and the letter's authors—poets largely from historically marginalized groups, who, he argued, had failed to criticize the Poetry Foundation's tokenism for years because they were the beneficiaries of the system.

He describes how celebrity, nepotism, and elitism informed the institutional culture of *Poetry* magazine and the Ruth Lilly Fellowship program, and how those who published in the magazine's pages participated in and perpetuated that culture in such a way that allowed the foundation to nominally support people of color while keeping its resources from the larger communities to which they belonged.

Williams writes powerfully about what reckoning with his own complicity with an unjust system feels like. "I cannot sign the original petition," he writes of the open letter, "because I already am a hypocrite and have only begun my journey to being a full ass, fallible person who has to accept all sides of this story, especially the ones that make me look and feel unworthy." When Williams grapples like this with his own position within the Poetry Foundation, it reminds me of how I felt in my classroom, agreeing wholeheartedly with my student's blistering critique of the Women's March, and having to admit to having gone there, and, worse, having felt meaning in it. Reading the letter, I am grateful for how Williams articulates the difficulty in calling for change when one is implicated in the very structures one wants to destroy, when one has compromised to the point of becoming the thing one hates. He writes: "How do you refashion the bones of a thing that suddenly has our face?"

And yet, the force and tone of his letter are not compromising. "No more insider bullshit," he writes in its final paragraph. "No more crews. Everything has to be open."

When he says this, I think of Harriet Monroe's Open Door policy. What would it look like for a magazine to be truly open? It would have to be free not only of indebtedness to specific movements or schools, but also of the kinds of *entangling alliances* that emerge quietly under the banner of liberalism, those that reward competition and the pursuit of individual success over a larger sense of collective well-being. And it's hard to imagine how such a magazine could coexist with a system that gives some organizations millions of dollars and others none, which is to say that it's hard to imagine the worst parts of liberalism fading without the inequities of capitalism also fading.

<><><>

We wrote a song for you to sing! my bandmates giddily declared one night as we set up for practice. The song was fast. Loud. It was nominally about George W. Bush, but it was really about all kinds of masculine violence. The lyrics were written in the persona of a terrifying, warmongering hypocrite.

The idea was that it would be subversive for such words to be sung by me, with my excessive eyeliner and booming Rickenbacker bass, with my too-long bangs and beat-up Chuck Taylors, with my white jeans and mutilated T-shirt that accentuated my breasts because of the way the words PORTLAND FUCKING OREGON strained across my chest.

We had a show that week at the Mercury Lounge, a test to see whether we could draw enough people to justify a monthly residency. Halfway through the set, it was my turn to sing. I rested my upper lip against the top of the mic and wailed,

> *i'm a crook i'm a thief in my veins you can see where the red and the blue collide*
> *singing hail to the chief as i bulldoze your street and you watch and you wave and you smile*
>
> *please don't be afraid 'cause god is on my side*
> *please don't make me wait lean back and open wiiiiide*

At the song's center was a chaotic breakdown: *i'm gonna be the one who loves you, i'm gonna be your man,* I was to sing in a low, seductive, macho moan. And then, a caterwauling transition back to the final verse: *i'm gonna push you to the ground and i will be your last man!*

It was my own personal "Welcome to the Jungle," misogynistic swagger and all.

And it was a perfect compromise. My bass line could be rough. Choppy. My vocals could be pitchy and the tempo could race.

It was what the song wanted. It showcased my unique talent. The crowd loved it. And I soaked up the shrieks and cheers as I tabulated the bodies in the room, the bar percentage, the merch we would sell.

3

COMPROMISER IN CHIEF

"A good compromise, a good piece of legislation, is like a good sentence," muses Barack Obama in 2004. He is eating lunch with William Finnegan of the *New Yorker*, who will write the first long-form profile of the future president. Miles Davis's *Kind of Blue* is playing in the background. As if inspired by the sound track, Obama nods and adds, "or a good piece of music. . . . Everybody can recognize it. They say, 'Huh. It works. It makes sense.'"

Reading the *New Yorker* piece now, four years after the end of the Obama presidency, I imagine the two men as they were in that inconceivably distant moment: Finnegan playing the handsome *New Yorker* journalist part, salt-and-pepper hair slightly mussed, probably wearing a dress shirt and jacket but no tie. The man Finnegan calls "Barack" is impossibly young, vibrating with energy, "lanky and dapper in a dark suit," equal parts invigorated and overwhelmed by his Senate campaign. He has just taken out a second mortgage on his apartment. The two eat lunch. I like to think that they bond over their mutual love of surfing.

Does it matter that the sound track for this conversation is *Kind of Blue*? In Finnegan's *New Yorker* piece, it is offered up merely as an atmospheric detail, but I am convinced that Obama really needs Miles Davis in that moment, as he searches for an analogy to the kind of legislative strategy he wants to pursue. This is because democratic politics is not really the most obvious scene for compromise. To the contrary, democratic politics is the domain that most depends upon disagreement and opposition. If you're looking for compromise, it's easier to find it in something that *everybody can recognize* because it's something that everybody likes. And what does everybody like?

Miles Davis's *Kind of Blue*. The best-selling jazz record of all time.

"Everyone, even people who say they don't like jazz, likes *Kind of Blue*," writes Fred Kaplan for *Slate*.

"Miles Davis's *Kind of Blue* belongs to that special class of album that everybody treasures immediately," writes Andy Battaglia for the usually skeptical *Pitchfork*. "Everybody likes it."

Everybody likes it? In my most adolescently oppositional moments, I have aspired to hating *Kind of Blue* just because of its seemingly unassailable likability. Yet I have to admit that I have more than once scrolled through my music library trying to find something to put on in the background during a dinner party and tapped *Kind of Blue* almost by instinct, grateful for an easy out.

Kind of Blue is a perfect dinner party sound track because it activates a feeling of nostalgia for a certain type of college-educated, left-leaning, dinner party–holding, *New Yorker*–reading kind of person. And nostalgia makes that kind of person feel comfortable because of one of the root words of nostalgia: *nostos*, a Greek term for an epic hero's return home. *Kind of Blue* lends the space it adorns a sense of home. *Everybody can recognize it. Everybody likes it.*

I can think through this intellectually, and yet I still marvel at how the first exchange of bass and piano on the album's opening track carries such powerful social magic. Those delicate, almost tentative plunkety-plunks; those two graceful answering chords. Somehow, that little phrase bonds. It unifies. It feels like a relic of a shared past.

It must have had this effect as it played in the background during that early interview, saturating the room with nostalgia as a young politician looked forward into a future he could not, at that early date, possibly imagine.

<><><>

What does it mean to compare a piece of legislation to a good sentence or a good song? Obama's analogy rests on the belief that good sentences and good songs often bring people together. That faced with a sentence or song that *everybody can recognize*, people will be more likely to put down their differences and focus on what they have in common. This belief about art's social power is not something that Obama made up. We have lots of stories about how art can help people get past seemingly intractable conflicts.

Take, for instance, a key moment in *Almost Famous*, a loosely autobiographical film written and directed by Cameron Crowe about his time spent as a teenage journalist for *Rolling Stone*. Crowe covered a number of bands, including Lynyrd Skynyrd, the Eagles, the Allman Brothers Band, and Led Zeppelin, during his time writing for the magazine. But in *Almost Famous*, Crowe's experiences are crystallized into a single fictional tour with a made-up rock band named Stillwater. This conflation allows for a heightening of stakes in the film, as the fate of Stillwater stands in for the fate of rock 'n' roll in general. If Stillwater survives, the film suggests, then rock will survive, and if rock survives, then something essential about human connection might stand a chance in the highly commercialized cultural landscape of the 1970s and beyond.

So it really matters when, late in the film, Stillwater looks like it will break up over a T-shirt.

The band is getting more famous, and as they do, their lead guitarist, Russell, begins to draw focus as Stillwater's charismatic icon. Then one day, their manager arrives with boxes full of their first official T-shirts. Without the band's knowledge, they have been printed to highlight Russell, while the rest of the band, including its front man, Jeff, are reduced to blurry shapes in the background.

Russell wants to brush it off as just a T-shirt. Jeff insists that it's more than that. The film runs through the argument quickly, focusing mostly on Jeff's jealousy and other pent-up emotional tensions among the bandmates. But Crowe's original screenplay for the film includes a longer version of the argument, in which the bandmates reflect on the relationship between their growing fame and their lack of creative control. Hollywood apparently didn't like Crowe's incursions into cultural critique. But I do.

"We have got to control what's happening to us," Jeff insists in Crowe's original script. "This is the slow-moving train of compromise that will *kill* us." Russell gets defensive. He insists that the T-shirt is nothing, that Jeff is just flying off the handle.

"Don't you see?" Jeff insists in response. "The t-shirt is *everything*. It's *everything*."

I want to take Jeff's side, particularly looking at the exchange from the vantage point of the late 1990s, when the screenplay was written. By then, the commodification of rock 'n' roll, which was always part of the genre and had accelerated in the 1970s, had become total. If the T-shirt symbolizes the end of rock music as a project of collective art-making that aspired to be to some degree outside of the market, then Jeff is absolutely right: the T-shirt is *everything*.

The next part is the same in the screenplay and in the film. Russell flees the scene. He finds a local house party. Drinks beer spiked with acid. Jumps, fully clothed, into a swimming pool, screaming, "I am a golden god!" The next morning, he climbs onto the school bus, wet, hungover, and still furious at Jeff. The band, it seems, is about to be destroyed by fame. And because this band is a stand-in for all bands, the possibility of finding meaning by creating music together looks like it might be finished, killed by a T-shirt.

The other bandmates and their entourage are sitting two to a seat, numbly staring off into space.

Elton John's "Tiny Dancer" plays mournfully over the bus's speakers.

And then, something incredible happens. One by one, they all begin to sing along.

The drummer taps his sticks on the seat back in front of him. The groupies know every word. Finally, even Jeff and Russell join in. *Hold me closer, tiny daaaaaaancer*, they croon.

By the end of the song, as if by magic, the fight is over. Russell will stay in the band. The tour will go on.

This scene is remembered perhaps more than any other in the film. It single-handedly elevated "Tiny Dancer," a minor single that garnered little attention in 1972, when it was originally released, and propelled it to gold, and then platinum, and then triple platinum status in the early 2000s.

I think that's because the scene offers its viewers something like a tiny utopia. If a bus full of angry people can, for just a moment, put aside their conflicts in favor of a collective experience of art, then maybe there is still a possibility for all of those grander utopian dreams: a community of humankind, the end of violence, of hatred, of war.

But there is a problem. Conflict isn't solved in this moment; it is merely ignored. The band's tensions can't possibly be reconciled by this sing-along, because the cause of their fight over the T-shirt—the relentless debasement of their art and social relationships with one another in the service of profit—has not been affected in the slightest. The band might overlook this particular T-shirt, but there will be other T-shirt moments.

The audience knows this, which is why the scene has such profound nostalgic force. That moment on the bus is so powerful because we have already seen the *slow-moving train of compromise* come for all rock bands, and the tiniest glimpse of the world before the arrival of that train is enough to convey a feeling of longing, a feeling that things could have been otherwise.

When Obama imagined that legislative compromise could be like a good song, I wonder if he had something like the "Tiny Dancer" scene in mind: a situation in which a piece of legislation would be so appealing that lawmakers could be temporarily shaken loose of their ossified positions. I can see how this vision could be compelling, because something analogous to that bus, if it happened in the Capitol, could actually accomplish something. If a sing-along is just a fleeting moment that will ultimately fade into nostalgia, passing a bill becomes law, so if you could get legislators to put aside their differing views, even for a moment, you could actually get something done.

In "My President Was Black," a retrospective essay on the Obama presidency published in the *Atlantic* in 2017, Ta-Nehisi Coates reads Obama's 2004 Democratic National Convention address as holding out hopes for precisely this kind of coming together. "By Obama's lights," Coates writes, "there was no liberal America, no conservative America, no black America, no white America, no Latino America, no Asian America, only 'the United States of America.'" The improbable success of Obama, his ability to win the presidency in a country that still carried the ideology of white supremacy in its structure and in the expressed beliefs of a significant portion of its population, was the result, Coates suggests, of a particular kind of optimism.

He doesn't put it this way, but Coates's analysis suggests that what Obama offered in that 2004 speech was something like the feeling of "Tiny Dancer": a sense of fundamental unity generated not by the real structures of experience, but by a story, a work of art, something that felt momentarily good enough for his audience to forget about very real conflicts. "Obama," Coates observes, "appealed to a belief in innocence—in particular a white innocence—that ascribed the country's historical errors more to misunderstanding and the work of a small cabal than to any deliberate malevolence or widespread racism." For a very brief moment, it looked as though America—white America and Black America; Democrats and Republicans—would sing along. "America was good," Coates writes, channeling Obama's optimism. "America was great."

But, Coates reminds us, "this speech ran counter to the history of the people it sought to address." And that history could not be resolved by a beautiful story. "American division," he writes, "was real."

This seems to be undeniably the case. And it's important to add that not only did Obama convey this optimism—his belief in the possibility that a divided country could be unified—in his emotional tenor and in the narratives he constructed, he also placed it at the core of his legislative strategy.

Consider, for instance, the Affordable Care Act (ACA), the policy that would be dubbed, first pejoratively by the right, and later with pride by the president himself, Obamacare. The policy was envisioned, from the start, as a compromise between the left and the right. Based on a plan that originated from a conservative think tank, the Heritage Foundation, and was first implemented by Republican governor Mitt Romney in Massachusetts, the ACA took a progressive priority—universal health care—and enacted it in a manner consistent with conservative principles. It not only maintained the private insurance market; it expanded that market by mandating that US taxpayers hold medical insurance and refraining from offering a public option. The ACA therefore was based on the belief that it would be possible to have it both ways: universal health care and the free market, a policy that by its very nature would be sure to appeal to both the left and the right. In this basic structure, the ACA was not unique. Obama's response to the recession included tax cuts for businesses and billions of dollars for large banks alongside a middle-class tax cut and funds for social services. He had other policy objectives that were similarly based on a vision of compromise, such as a cap-and-trade market for carbon emissions and immigration reform that would both increase spending on border security and provide a pathway to citizenship. Ironically, the only compromises Obama was able to move through the legislative branch were the ones he was able to introduce under Democratic control of both the Senate and the House, which ended soon after the ACA was signed into law.

There is a difference between the emotional force of the Obama of the 2004 Democratic National Convention address and the pragmatic rationality of the Obama of the ACA proposal. The former is exemplary of Obama's notorious charm, his charisma, his capacity to, as one Illinois Republican says of Obama in Finnegan's article, make people who disagree with him still *like* him. The latter is an example of another cluster of observations frequently made about Obama: it is an example of his pragmatism, his interest in the practical politics of compromise, his wonky interest in the minutiae of law and legislative policy.

But these two sides of the former president—one emotional, one rational; one based on narrative and performance, the other based on logistics and policy—both were harnessed at times to serve a single purpose: the imagined unification of divided interests among the American public. A public united in hope and optimism; a public that sees that its interests can be compatible after all. This was the Obama promise.

This is why I think Obama's comparison of a good legislative compromise to a good sentence or a good song is important. It suggests a specific notion of compromise: one that is grounded both in mutual interest and in mutual appreciation. One that both sides will experience as both logical and pleasurable.

Obama was not alone in thinking such a thing was possible. His success reflected his exceptional abilities as a speaker and strategist, but it also stemmed from a general belief in the desirability of third ways and compromises, one that was pervasive in center-left thinking throughout the '90s and '00s in the United States and in Europe in the administrations of Bill Clinton, Tony Blair, Gerhard Schroeder, and others. These administrations all functioned differently in their various contexts, but they each presumed to some degree that ideological divisions between left and right—divisions premised during the twentieth century on the existence of socialism as a meaningful alternative to capitalism—were no longer relevant in the post–Cold War age. Unlike their more draconian neoliberal forebears like Ronald Reagan and Margaret Thatcher, who earned a reputation for merely tearing down social services, wage protections, and publicly funded social institutions, these "Third Way" figures believed that the free market could be harnessed to provide social welfare. The war that existed between the appeal to large government social interventions—an appeal grounded in the ideology of socialism—and free market individualism was one that they believed could be reconciled through compromise.

But not a sad compromise, not a begrudging compromise: the compromise of Third Way and center-left thinking was a utopian compromise, one based on the belief that there need not be meaningful opposition between commitment to the free market and commitment to human thriving, between the interests of the individual and the interests of the collective.

Just like a good sentence or a good song, legislative compromises, they imagined, could be beautiful.

Maybe this is why Democrats were so surprised by the unwillingness of Republicans to sing along with Obama's legislative agenda, but that's what happened. It's as if the Democratic Party launched into an inspiring chorus of "Tiny Dancer," motioning encouragingly to their colleagues on the other side of the aisle to join them, and the Republicans responded with crossed arms and glares, mumbling, "I hate this song."

Coates's assessment of this moment is simple. Obama's fatal flaw, he argues, was his underestimation of American racism, and therefore his tendency to "underestimate his opposition's resolve to destroy him."

I agree. Racism certainly fed the right's refusal to compromise with the Obama administration. But it wasn't just racism that led to this state of affairs; it was also a problem with the way centrist policy makers envisioned the dynamics of compromise and power.

A compromise is not a compromise when it is offered up, fully formed, in advance. No matter how much it seems to be something *everybody can recognize*, there will always be curmudgeons who refuse to like the thing that everyone else does, who want to hate the thing they know they're expected to like.

"Governing a democracy without compromise is impossible," write Amy Gutmann and Dennis Thompson in their book *The Spirit of Compromise*. This may be true. If a plurality of voices is admitted into political decision-making, there will be situations in which some positions are essentially incompatible with others. And in those situations, there are two options: compromise or the overriding of the weaker party by the stronger one. So despite my dispositional aversion to the concept of compromise in general, I understand that practically speaking, it is sometimes necessary to make compromises.

To say that the process of coming to a compromise is necessary, however, does not mean that the outcome of compromises will be pleasurable, likable, predictable, or recognizable, definitely not to everyone and maybe not to anyone.

I believe that compromises are ugly things and that they should display their ugliness for everyone to see. They should hold themselves up and say: *This is what you get when you give up your ideals. You get a policy that skimps on justice. You get a stopgap measure that will fail long term. You get a program that you wanted without the funding to support it. You get an inch or two in the direction of what is right.*

When I say compromises are ugly things, I don't mean that they are monstrous or oppositional or disturbing or challenging. I mean that they are unsatisfying, awkward, boring, haphazard. They might be the best we can get, but they do not and should not please us. Compromises are not like a good sentence or a good song. To imagine that they could be like either of these things is to unreasonably elevate compromise and diminish art.

I say that Obama needed Miles Davis's *Kind of Blue* in that critical moment in his interview with Finnegan, that he found in the album a metaphor for legislation that he hoped could transcend political divisions by being universally recognizable, by seeming to *just work*. As a cultural touchstone, *Kind of Blue* serves as the perfect example of the most pleasurable kind of compromise, the kind that everyone can embrace, if only as background music.

But it is ironic that Miles Davis was recruited for this task, the musician who perhaps most fervently opposed compromises, who stridently disavowed his own work once it became easily digestible. For example, in a 1986 interview with Ben Sidran, Davis said of *Kind of Blue*, "I have no feel for it anymore."

Why? Because the album has become "like warmed-over turkey," Davis explains.

This comment is characteristic of Davis, who dramatically reinvented himself—and his work—multiple times over, rejecting his past accomplishments in favor of what he could try next. Davis's irreverence toward his previous body of work was in marked disregard for what he knew would work for his fans. Davis could have recorded bebop album after bebop album and still would have had a successful career. He could have done the same thing with the modal experiments that blossomed into *Kind of Blue*. But instead he moved on to albums like *Bitches Brew*. Inspired by funk and rock 'n' roll, he turned away from what could even be called jazz at the time in favor of hybrid experiments with electric instrumentation, genre mixing, ambient textures, and abrasive, almost atonal, improvisations.

Davis is often called an iconoclast, and he is compared to other artists, such as Picasso, who destroyed the very schools of art they themselves advanced. As critic Anton Spice puts it, "For many Miles fans [*Bitches Brew*] was a line in the sand, for everyone else it was more like a meteorite destroying the whole beach."

The irony is this: As the grandfather of the hybrid form "jazz-fusion," Miles Davis brought together seemingly incompatible schools and methods, such as rock and jazz; electric and acoustic instrumentation; improvisation and advanced tape editing. And bringing two elements together that seem as if they are incompatible and showing how they work together seems like the definition of compromise. But there is a difference between compromises that are imagined to be stabilizing and those that are imagined to be destabilizing.

When artworks compromise, they often do so in order to challenge norms, to put disparate styles in relation to one another in order to generate tension, to put focus on the edges among those styles, to push back against orthodoxies. But those compromises are often interpreted by listeners, critics, and scholars as signaling not tension, but compatibility. I call this interpretation of stylistic hybridity—the belief that works of art can reconcile tensions between marketability and experimentation, between the popular and the avant-garde—*compromise aesthetics*. By perpetuating the belief that stylistic differences can be easily reconciled, compromise aesthetics can erase what often makes hybrid works interesting in the first place: their performance of disjunction, dissent, conflict.

Something similar happens in discussions of political compromises. When political compromises are imagined to be appealing to everyone in advance, they erase what is most promising but also most difficult about the democratic political process: the struggle with disparate points of view, clashes among individuals and groups representing opposing interests, grappling with differences in power, and the formation and undermining of hierarchies.

I perform exactly this kind of erasure when I use Miles Davis's work as a dinner party sound track. I choose it because it is stable. Recognizable. Predictable. I am using it not for its innovations in form, but for its regressive nostalgic power.

The compromises that motivated Davis were the ones that would challenge the very notion of *nostos*, that would make rock fans wonder what "rock" even meant and make jazz fans entertain the possibility that rock, that corporate genre, might have something to offer experimental music. And the consequences of those compromises, beyond their destruction of conventional categories, could never be known in advance.

In 2017, Elton John released the first official music video for "Tiny Dancer." The video features many different people in many different cars all over Los Angeles singing along with the song. There is a Latina woman driving a vintage Volvo with an urn of ashes in the passenger seat, a skateboarding teenager singing along to her oversize earphones on a commuter train, a group of friends singing in a hotboxed car, their faces almost obscured by thick smoke. And in an inexplicable cameo, there is goth-industrial singer Marilyn Manson, sitting in the driver's seat of a camper van, lovingly stroking an enormous yellow snake.

In an interview with *Campaign* about the making of the video, its director, Max Weiland, who was born well after the song's 1972 release, explains that his vision for the piece came from his sense of the song as a "classic driving song." This connection between the song and the road undoubtedly stems from its appearance in the bus scene of *Almost Famous*. The persistence of this connection over time suggests that the scene in the film is unusually "sticky," that it has managed to conspicuously adhere to a portion of the public, even those who likely did not experience firsthand either the song or *Almost Famous* at the time of their release.

In *The Cultural Politics of Emotion*, Sara Ahmed argues that sticky objects are those that take on emotion as they move from person to person, gathering histories—both real and imagined—and dense, often hidden, associations that carry with them intense feelings. What sticks, she suggests, is not so much the work itself, but the feelings that become attached to the work.

In the case of the "Tiny Dancer" scene, those feelings seem to revolve around a deep sense of nostalgia. By this I do not mean only that the scene is nostalgic for an idealized 1970s, with its bell-bottoms and headbands and moccasins and starry-eyed, long-haired dreamers. If this was the case, we would expect to see Weiland's video take up the same time period. Instead, I mean that the emotion that the "Tiny Dancer" scene circulates, evokes, and deepens is the feeling of nostalgia itself. And this makes sense, because sing-alongs are nostalgic events almost by default. Their existence is predicated upon a group of people unified through a shared past as it is embodied in a song.

Film theorist Svetlana Boym argues that nostalgia is significant in contemporary art because it does more than signal a relationship to a past. It also provides a site for utopian thinking in a moment when future utopias seem inaccessible, outdated, or unbelievable. She writes, "Nostalgia itself has a utopian dimension, only it is no longer directed toward the future."

This explains why the "Tiny Dancer" scene would offer such a compelling utopian vision. Its nostalgia is attached not to the 1970s, because there was clearly no utopia to be had during that decade of disappointment, but to the notion of coming together, of putting conflict aside, of singing along. It locates that utopia, crucially, in the past.

And this is where the problem arises. When nostalgia anchors its utopianism in the past, it tends to be conservative. Furthermore, there is always the danger that the *nostos* that gives nostalgia its emotional power becomes attached to the desire to return not to an actual home or historical past, but to an invented one. "The danger of nostalgia," Boym warns, "is that it tends to confuse the actual home and the imaginary one." *Almost Famous* is about this confusion, about how difficult it is to parse the distinction as it existed during the moment of 1970s rock 'n' roll, a moment that was already nostalgic about itself.

The distinction between a real home and an invented one is crystallized in the film when, as the busload of musicians and groupies belt out "Tiny Dancer," fifteen-year-old William, a cipher for Cameron Crowe himself, insists, "I *have* to go home." William has joined the tour to interview Stillwater for *Rolling Stone*. It was supposed to be a brief trip. But he has missed days of school. His mother, frantic on the phone, begs him with increasing urgency to come back. All he needs is a few minutes to interview the band, but he keeps getting put off.

"Sh," says the groupie queen, Penny Lane, waving her fingers in front of his face. "You are home." Penny lays her head on William's shoulder. He faces the camera. His expression is hard to read. Is it confusion? Shock? Temptation? Epiphany?

Penny embodies the myth of the rock 'n' roll life on the road. And in this moment, William seems as if he might be ready to believe in it. But the film will end in disappointment. William will ultimately choose his real home and his real mother, the fantasy of the endless rock tour receding on the horizon.

Boym argues that there is a bigger danger than this sweet, if sad, nostalgic fantasy. "In extreme cases," she writes, nostalgia "can create a phantom homeland, for the sake of which one is ready to die or kill."

I recently learned that Donald Trump plays "Tiny Dancer" at his campaign rallies. Cultural critics have marveled at this choice, given that Elton John's queerness would seem to be in contradiction to the homophobic policies that Trump often openly espouses at these rallies. But perhaps it is this notion of the phantom homeland, this regressive version of *nostos*, that allows the song to somehow fit Trump's conservative appeal to Make America Great Again.

Did we ever sing along? Has legislation ever been something that *everybody can recognize*? If the threat from the far right comes from the creation of a *phantom homeland* in a white America that never existed, the threat from the center-left might be the belief that once upon a time compromises were beautiful. Prepared in advance. Appreciated like works of art. And while the left is by no means ready to die or to kill for that lost sense of home, the belief that this home once existed squanders other political possibilities.

Despite all of this, I still get weepy during the "Tiny Dancer" scene of *Almost Famous*. Watching the 2017 video made me realize why. My nostalgia is activated not by the song's ability to bring people together, but by the fact that all of those people were on the bus in the first place. In the 2017 video, those who are singing along are all in separate cars, by themselves, or isolated by headphones on public transportation. They are alone or in groups according to predictable markers: couples or friends who look alike. The message of the video is that the fact that they are all singing along to "Tiny Dancer" at the same time, despite their distance, is bringing them together through some kind of alchemical magic of simultaneity. But, in reality, it's not. They do not encounter one another. They remain with their people, or they remain alone.

Boym observes that the word *nostalgia* comes from *nostos*, but also *algia*, which means pain, pain that Boym associates with longing for things to be different. The longing of nostalgia, she suggests, is what gives the feeling its utopian dimension. And longing together, longing collectively, can potentially be marshaled toward the construction of new, unexpected futures.

My longing is attached to the possibility of solidarity, of meaningful connections that are not just metaphorical, but material. I long for a bus full of people earnestly engaged in a collective attempt to undo the arbitrary hierarchies of fame and inherited privilege; to challenge exploitation and injustice; to imagine a better way of organizing ourselves. We would, I imagine, often be fighting. But when I think about the promise of democracy, it is that image that comes to mind.

4

HER HAND ON MY OCTAVE

"I loathe compromise," writes Margaret Anderson in a 1916 editorial for her arts and literary magazine, the *Little Review*. The magazine, now best known as the first periodical to publish parts of James Joyce's *Ulysses*, was initially imagined as a vehicle for Anderson's commitment to challenging mainstream tastes. Along with her partner and lover, Jane Heap, Anderson published anarchist political tracts, work by Dadaists and surrealists, and experimental writing by Sherwood Anderson, Wallace Stevens, and H.D., among others.

Anderson loathed compromise in editorial work, in art, and in politics. This was the high point of avant-gardism and school-based writing; compromise was not yet a formal tendency in works of art themselves. But she still saw compromise all around her in the mandate that people, especially women, be even-toned, moderate, and reasonable. Anderson did not want to be reasonable. Writing on feminism in the magazine's pages, she proclaimed that "a clear-thinking magazine can have only one attitude; the degree of ours is ardent!"

Ardor characterizes Anderson's tone, but it also becomes a value in and of itself in her editorial work. "I loathe compromise, and yet I have been compromising in every issue by putting in things that were 'almost good' or 'interesting enough' or 'important,'" she writes in this particular issue. "There will be no more of it."

Against "good poems" she wants to publish capital-*A* Art, art that goes beyond simply being the best version of itself. Notably diverging from *Poetry* magazine's Open Door policy, Anderson believed that truly great art was not a matter of individual quality; it was a matter of ferocity of commitment. She wanted art that could knock a person over, art that "uses up all the life it can get." She invokes the modernist credo "art for art's sake," but in an avant-garde reversal insists that this means not a retreat from the world of politics and history but a commitment to it. "Revolution *is* Art," she explains. "You want free people just as you want the Venus that was modelled by the sea."

She ends her editorial with a threat: "If there is only one really beautiful thing for the September number it shall go in and the other pages will be left blank."

She meant it. The September 1916 issue of the *Little Review* includes thirteen blank pages.

Decisions like this meant that in the early years of the *Little Review*, Anderson was often broke. Her uncompromising stances didn't play well with funders, who didn't want ads for their products appearing alongside paeans to Nietzschean ethics and radical feminism, or placed in issues with mostly blank pages. Evicted from her apartment and then from the magazine's offices, she even slept in a tent on the shores of Lake Michigan for a period of time.

But, as I have come to learn—because these are the kinds of details you always learn about female literary celebrities—her hair was always perfectly done; her suit always clean and flawless. "I possessed one blouse, one hat and one tailored suit," she writes in her autobiography. "The blouse could be made to serve two days. Then I washed it—by moonlight or by sunrise. Being of crêpe georgette it didn't need to be ironed."

After storms along the lakeside that would leave her drenched, Anderson writes, she would "squeeze a few buckets of water from my suit, pat it gently into shape, hang it on a cord in my tent and go downtown the next morning looking immaculate."

In the Wikipedia entry devoted to Anderson, I find this choice phrase highlighted in the center of the page, written by Ben Hecht, a writer she knew:

> It was surprising to see a coiffure so neat on a noggin so stormy.

It's utterly predictable and awful that this brilliant thinker would be characterized by her hairstyle, and yet I'm not sure Anderson would have objected, attesting in her autobiography to the "tributes without which I could not live: You look so beautifully groomed!"

I'm oddly grateful for this description. I feel as if I can picture Anderson calmly pinning up her hair in whatever mirror she could find, having slept in her tent the night before. Perhaps she is in the bathroom of a lakeside restaurant? In the ladies' lounge in a downtown hotel? At a cosmetics counter in Marshall Field's department store? Perhaps she gazes at her hairline in the cracked—no, it would never be cracked—*polished* mirror of her own tiny compact?

Do her hands shake? And if they do, is it out of financial worry or rage toward some political or aesthetic position with which she vehemently disagrees? From what I have learned about Anderson, it could easily be either.

She has become a totem that I invoke on mornings when, after a brief and thin sleep, I twist loops of hair onto the top of my head and pin them with trembling fingers.

It occurs to me that many of my friends are Anderson's progeny: stormy-nogginned women whose overall comportments are carefully composed in direct proportion to their anger, their desperation, their fear, their drive.

A neat coiffure and a stormy noggin. This is a pairing of two disparate traits. The neat coiffure masks the stormy noggin to some degree.

Maybe as a matter of survival. Maybe as a matter of social strategy. Is it a compromise?

If it is, it is not the kind of compromise that turns conflict into a sad peace.

I find myself looking to Anderson, saint of ardor, revolutionary in crêpe georgette, to learn how to survive in this world, as a woman, as a critic, as a friend and a partner, with this stormy noggin that I cannot seem to hide or tame no matter how carefully I comport myself, no matter how many times I stand at the mirror and beg the flashing-eyed reflection to *just try for once, please try to stay calm, to be nice, to fit in.*

Eighty years after Anderson washed her blouses by moonlight, David Foster Wallace, squirming in discomfort on *The Charlie Rose Show*, would offer this explanation for the nearly one hundred pages of endnotes in his mammoth novel, *Infinite Jest*:

> I . . . am constantly on the lookout for ways to fracture the text that aren't totally disoriented. . . . There's got to be some interplay between how difficult you make it for the reader and how seductive it is for the reader so the reader's willing to do it. The endnotes were, for me, a useful compromise.

In Wallace's terms, compromise is a negotiation between *how difficult you make it for the reader and how seductive it is for the reader*. It's a formal method aimed at expanding an audience while retaining interest and novelty as aesthetic goals. It's a gesture that looks democratic, welcoming in a broader audience than experimental fiction would generally allow.

But this begs the question: What kind of difficulty will this reader consent to and still allow herself to be seduced? Fragmented syntax? Fractured narratives? Will she accept 100 pages of endnotes? What will it take to seduce her into reading a 1,079-page novel?

"Feminists are always saying this," Wallace interjects when he's asked, in the Charlie Rose interview, about the length of *Infinite Jest*. "Feminists are saying white males say, 'Okay, I'm going to sit down and write this enormous book and impose my phallus on the consciousness of the world.'"

Wallace shakes his head. Blinks.

"And you say?" Rose prods, generously.

"I . . . I . . . if that was going on, it was going on on a level of awareness I do *not* want to have access to," Wallace replies with a look of disgust.

It makes sense that Rose, who we now know had a habit of stroking the upper thighs of his female coworkers without their consent, would want to change the subject. But I am still surprised when he responds with this probing follow-up: "Do you still play tennis?"

The "feminists" Wallace was referring to may have included Michiko Kakutani, who objected to the length of *Infinite Jest* in her review in the *New York Times*. His response is telling:

"If the length seems gratuitous, as it did to a very charming Japanese lady from the *New York Times*, then one arouses ire. I'm aware of that."

Literary scholar Amy Hungerford quotes this response as part of a lengthy chronicle of Wallace's misogyny, including his abusive treatment of the writer Mary Karr. Hungerford argues that Wallace's conduct in relation to women is relevant to a reading of his fiction because he himself conceived of the relationship between himself and the reader as sexual. It wasn't only on *Charlie Rose* that he used the language of seduction to describe the author-reader dynamic. As Hungerford points out, in an early short story an author figure observes that a good story should "treat the reader like it wants to . . . well, fuck him."

"Wallace proposes to fuck me," Hungerford concludes. "Unlike the 'charming Japanese lady' whose job it was to review *Infinite Jest* for the *Times*, I can refuse the offer, and so I will."

I quote Hungerford not to agree with her decision not to read *Infinite Jest*, nor to complain about the length of the book. I myself have been successfully seduced by Wallace's novel, and I do not regret the experience. But I quote her to point out that the defense of aesthetic compromise in the name of what will successfully seduce the reader assumes a lot about that reader and what she may or may not be into.

Hungerford, for one, has an account of the reader that Wallace successfully seduces: the self-satisfied lit bro, eager to demonstrate his stamina and intelligence. "The book's marketers were smart," she writes. "They knew their audience and what kind of dare would provoke them: Are you smart enough and strong enough—indeed, are you man enough—to read a genius's thousand-page novel?"

I would add that this marketing campaign is not simply reliant upon what she calls "a Jurassic vision of literary genius." That Jurassic vision gave us a different set of incredibly long, incredibly difficult books. *Ulysses. Gravity's Rainbow. The Tunnel.*

Wallace's is a new version of that kind of book, one that markets itself as a compromise. You can both feel smart *and* be entertained, *Infinite Jest* insists. Yes, the novel does pitch itself as a dare, as a test of intelligence, but as Wallace says in the Rose interview, the novel is careful to provide enough readerly gratification, payoff, and pleasure that it can be successfully marketed to a mass—albeit disproportionately white and male—audience.

<><><>

What changed between Anderson's time and our own that would make a book like *Infinite Jest*—a book that styles itself as both experimental masterpiece and accessible pop sensation—desirable, let alone possible? What ushered in a decade in which literary fiction was dominated by such books, books by Dave Eggers, Jennifer Egan, Jonathan Safran Foer, Zadie Smith, Michael Chabon, and many other authors who produced formally innovative yet digestible works of fiction at the turn of the twenty-first century?

This turn was initiated by a new generation of writers in the 1990s who were educated during a highly polarized moment in literary culture. On the one hand, there were the experimentalists of the 1960s and '70s: Language poets and postmodernists. These writers saw aesthetic difficulty and novelty as the hallmark of literary excellence and, in the case of the Language poets, as modes of political refusal. On the other hand, there were the traditionalists, the conservative New Formalists, the Garrison Keillor populists, and the proponents of MFA programs, which were then perceived to be grooming grounds for traditional, antiexperimental, marketable products.

The new generation of writers was frustrated by the limitations of these two positions, and as a result rejected the notion that formally inventive literature requires intentional opposition to the norms of mainstream writing and the expectations of mainstream audiences. As Stephanie Burt explains, by the early '90s, young writers "sought something new: something more open to personal emotion, to story and feeling, than Language poetry, but more complicated intellectually than most of the creative-writing programs' poets allowed." Compromise was born as a solution to polarization.

But this version of the story neglects to mention something else that was happening during the 1990s, something that Wallace himself was thinking a lot about. In the 1990s it became more difficult to think of literature as having autonomy from the influence of the market. This was because of changes in art and media—Wallace, for instance, writes

extensively about the effect that television has on literary audiences—
but it was also because of changes in economics.

Neoliberal economic policies—policies that were driven toward the ex-
pansion of the free market into spheres of life that were not previously
subject to market forces—were initially instituted in the United States
by the Reagan administration, in the 1980s. But once the Clinton
administration took up the mantle of neoliberal reforms and doubled
down on those policies, neoliberalization began to look like a permanent state of affairs that would not be challenged. The dissolution of the
Soviet Union only furthered this belief, as socialism both domestically
and geopolitically no longer appeared to offer either a threat or an alternative to global capitalism. The consequence of this was a general sense
that, as neoliberal ideologue Margaret Thatcher put it, there was "no
alternative" to the competitive forces of the market.

Neoliberalism was becoming more than a set of policies; it was changing the horizon of expectations for individuals in a range of activities.
As institutions were explicitly privatized or made to adhere to free
market principles, it became harder to imagine that one's activities
could meaningfully resist the market. This was true in literary culture
as well, as many small publishers disappeared or were brought under
the umbrella of large publishers, and as large publishers became international conglomerates that managed hundreds of imprints, some of
them operating with relative autonomy but most of them functioning
with the expectation that they would need to give a bottom-line rationale for their editorial choices.

Some independent presses—FC2, Coffee House Press, Dalkey Archive,
Graywolf Press, Grove Atlantic, and New Directions, among others—
did survive as alternatives to what was once known as "the big six"
and is now, with the 2013 merger of Penguin and Random House, "the
big five." And, as many are nonprofits, they have continued to publish work that is not driven exclusively toward sales. Some divisions
in large publishing houses also continue to operate without producing
enormous profits; they exist primarily to give the press prestige. But

between the ideology of neoliberalism that offers up the free market as the model for all activities and the material effects of the changing publishing industry, literature was increasingly subject to the calculus of sales figures and audience.

Of course, writers want to get paid. The starving artist is a myth that has always served the privileged. Literary culture was never a meritocracy; standards of judgment have always been shaped by social hierarchies including class, gender, and race. It is also the case that the avant-garde has always been attached to the ruling class "by an umbilical cord of gold," as Clement Greenberg observed in 1939. But despite this attachment, avant-garde movements once could have aspirations to exist outside of the capitalist market; they could therefore see their activities, however idealistically, as challenging to the status quo. Compromise aesthetics take root when the notion of radicalism in art starts to seem naive, as it does now, even to its once most passionate advocates; when art's inextricability from capitalism is used as evidence by scholars, critics, and practitioners alike to argue that anything like an avant-garde refusal is at best ridiculous and at worst disingenuous.

In that context, someone like Wallace, who openly discussed the role of aesthetic compromises in making his work marketable, no longer seemed like a sellout in a world in which selling out was inevitable. He just seemed reasonable, democratic, sensible. He just seemed like a good compromiser.

In 1918, the *Little Review* adopted this subtitle:

MAKING NO COMPROMISE WITH THE PUBLIC TASTE

It has been suggested that the tagline was the creation of Ezra Pound, who joined the magazine's editorial board that year and who was known for his profound hostility toward mass culture, a hostility that ultimately manifested in his fascist politics. And the slogan does sound Poundian: brutal, snooty, and pretentious.

But Anderson's distrust of compromise preceded her formal association with Pound and was expressed, in the early years of the magazine, in a markedly different manner than that of the modernist elite.

For Pound, *making no compromise* meant publishing a specific coterie of writers. "I want a place where I and T. S. Eliot can appear once a month," he proposed to Anderson prior to joining the *Little Review* as the magazine's foreign correspondent. "And where Joyce can appear when he likes, and where Wyndham Lewis can appear if he comes back from the war. DEFINITELY a place for our regular appearance and where our friends and readers (what few of 'em there are), can look with assurance of finding us."

When the *Little Review* began, however, it envisioned itself not as a coterie publication but as a radically open one. In the magazine's first issue, Anderson writes to her readers, "If you've ever read poetry with a feeling that it was your religion, your very life . . . if you've ever felt music replacing your shabby soul with a new one of shining gold . . . if these things have happened to you and continue to happen till you're left quite speechless with the wonder of it all, then you'll understand our hope to bring them nearer to the common experience of the people who read us."

Anderson imagines art as something that could be brought close to everyday experience, something that could enrich seemingly mundane activities. And it's possible that this notion—the belief that a deep concern for art could be accessed by people of all kinds—motivated one of the *Little Review*'s most unique features: The Reader Critic.

The section, which appeared in most issues, consisted of a cluster of letters, often framed with editorial commentary. It was intended to be, as the scholar Alan Golding describes it, "another space . . . in which difference can circulate." It showcased letters from a staggering range of readers. In the first appearance of the section, in 1914, one could read a letter from Emma Goldman alongside a letter from someone simply referred to as "A Boy Reader, Chicago." Midwestern women without significant formal education found their letters side by side with those of coastal literary luminaries. And while the positions taken in the letters were sometimes critical and sometimes affirmative, they were always intensely passionate, modeling the enthusiasm that Anderson valued.

An antipathy to compromise, particularly in the early years of the magazine, did not mean closing ranks or being hostile to the public. But it did mean shying away from moderation, understood as much as an affect or tone as a practice.

In this period that saw a proliferation of -isms throughout the art world in the United States and Europe, the *Little Review* was avowedly not a partisan magazine; it did not ally itself with a specific aesthetic school. And yet, unlike *Poetry*, which saw itself as ideally a neutral space for excellent work, the *Little Review* displayed a strong editorial hand. Anderson often framed texts with her own commentary, which tended to be passionate, argumentative, effusive, and sometimes even directly critical of the texts she included in the magazine's pages.

In her editorial on the magazine's first year in press, Anderson writes that she had received letters accusing the magazine of being "uncritical, indiscriminate, juvenile, exuberant, chaotic, amateurish, emotional, tiresomely enthusiastic, and a lot of other things . . . that are usually said about faulty new undertakings." She cites the criticisms of readers who see the magazine as lacking a specific focus, argument, intention, or position. And ultimately, she agrees with them. A good magazine, she argues, "should suggest, not conclude . . . should stimulate to thinking rather than dictate thought."

But lest we think that Anderson means this approach to lead to the valuing of compromising discourse of any kind, she reminds her readers of her first priority: felt intensity.

"I should rather be an extremist," she writes in the same editorial, "than a—well, it's scarcely a matter of choice: people are either extremists or nonentities; I should far rather sense the big things about a cause or character even vaguely than to analyze its little qualities quite clearly; in short, I should rather feel a great deal and know a little than feel a little and know a lot."

Making no compromise, for Anderson, is not the same thing as the smug elitism of Pound and his ilk. It is not the same thing as devotion to a specific form of avant-gardism. Or stable partisanship. It doesn't mean shutting out conflicting points of view. To the contrary: it means valuing extremity in oneself and in others; it means being willing to take strong positions and then, when one is moved to do so, to change one's mind and take other strong positions. It means seeing conflict as generative. And it means seeking it out in many directions, among friends and enemies, established artists and amateurs.

I agree with this version of *making no compromise*. Being uncompromising can seem like a form of self-righteousness, but Anderson's difference from Pound demonstrates that refusing compromise as an ethos, tone, or style can still allow for intellectual generosity. Taking strong positions and being argumentative can paradoxically provide opportunities to be open to the ideas of others and accept that one is wrong.

Nevertheless, this trait of Anderson's was often misunderstood. She writes in her autobiography, "I had always been confronted with people who found my zest for argument disagreeable, who said they lost interest in any subject the moment it became controversial. My answer had been that argument wasn't necessarily controversy."

"I had never been able to understand why people dislike to be challenged," she continues. "For me challenge has always been the great impulse, the only liberation."

Reading Anderson contending with the dissonance between her own *zest for argument* and the response she received from those around her has the sudden effect of reshuffling a set of memories from my life, beginning in childhood and reaching to the present, in which friends or acquaintances wear inexplicable expressions of hurt. Or shock. Or nervous tension.

I have learned, over time, to read these expressions as indicating that I have been antagonistic rather than inviting and that I have been read as hostile, critical, even mean.

My sister has suggested that we institute a safe word that she can invoke when I've turned the corner from a robust debate to a systematic demolishing of my interlocutor's point of view. One of my closest friends once jokingly said that if there was a bingo game based on spending an evening with me, the center square would read SMASHES BELIEF THAT YOU HOLD DEAR.

The other night it happened among a group of parents working toward greater racial and economic equity in the St. Louis Public Schools. We were tired and depressed following a meeting in which we were told that any significant redistribution of resources among the district's schools was impossible.

We all clustered in the hallway under sad fluorescent lights. It was late. I stepped into a conversation among a small group of white women, who were talking about how the failure of the district to respond to our demands meant that we should *focus on working on ourselves*. As the fire of our arguments with the district leadership faded, I felt that familiar white-woman affect, self-righteous *niceness*, taking hold. One suggested a reading group. There was a general murmur of approval.

Another raised her chin and said, *the problem is that some people are self-ish.* A third declared, *the solution can only start with us; we need to talk about how we raise our kids.* I could feel my face get hot and my hands begin to shake. I saw our demands for better policies slowly mutating into a project of moralizing and personal self-searching. And then I behaved badly.

I said something about how noxious it is when morality overtakes politics, about how ineffectual it is to replace a call for structural change with a call for better behavior. At the moment, I was honestly trying to contribute to the conversation, but the looks on the faces of the other parents told me that what I had offered wasn't a contribution. It was an imperious, critical rant.

So I went home and felt crappy and embarrassed. And I wrote more than one apology note on Facebook Messenger that probably made the situation worse.

I deeply admire your personal choices, but . . . , one began.

Now at the close of my fourth decade of living, I have learned to endure this pattern: a lively discussion; a sudden silence; those faces; and then, later, shame.

Anderson writes of Jane Heap that there was a phrase she used "as a tribute to someone who (briefly) understood her": "a hand on the exact octave that is me."

As I read how Anderson contended with the effects of her combative social instinct, I feel her hand on my octave. It calms my rising heartbeat, blots out the images of shocked and hurt expressions on the faces of my friends. My breathing slows. I feel her slender fingers. Their cold pressure. Their unyielding weight.

<><><>

In a recent lecture, modernist scholar Alan Golding argues that the hostility of some of Anderson's editorial remarks toward the readers who contributed to The Reader Critic section "consciously sets *The Little Review* against the democratic view of audience projected in *Poetry* magazine's epigraph, Whitman's 'to have great poets, there must be great audiences, too.'" This epigraph reflects *Poetry* magazine's attitude toward its audience, one of generosity and welcome that stood in some distinction to the *Little Review*'s sometimes-aggressive attitude toward its audience.

But this seems to me to be a misreading. Not of the *Little Review*, which Golding knows better than perhaps any other living scholar, but of democracy. Democracy does not require neutrality; it requires equality of access. And equality of access does not mean each position is treated as if it has the same inherent worth.

I would argue that, in publishing positions with which the editors disagree, and then, yes, sometimes responding to those positions with passionate bile, the *Little Review* took its audience every bit as seriously as *Poetry* does its audience. In fact, one could say that in contending with the polarizing positions of members of its audience, it took them *more* seriously.

A similar misreading of democracy continues to afflict judgments about today's aesthetics. In David St. John's introduction to the 2009 *American Hybrid: A Norton Anthology of New Poetry*, he writes that the "most compelling poetry" beginning in the 1990s "has ignored and/or defied categorization." These works embrace hybrid forms; they stage compromises among previously opposed styles, schools, and aesthetic values.

The motivation for the anthology is the celebration of this aesthetic sensibility. But its aspirations and justifications lean, at times, toward the political, finding justification in the language of democracy.

St. John writes that he and his coeditor, Cole Swensen, chose not to highlight the work of any particular writers in their introductions because it would be "antithetical to both the project and spirit of this anthology" to suggest that one poet "can be judged as 'better' or 'more important' than any other." *American Hybrid*, he writes, is based on "the idea of an American poetry based upon plurality, not purity."

These statements fall in line with Golding's presumed concept of democratic aesthetics: the notion that a more welcoming, inclusive, plural, and unified approach to art either implicitly or explicitly models a better and more democratic political sphere.

Put simply, the thesis is this: art and art venues that make themselves widely available to a general audience and treat that audience with tolerance and respect are more democratic than those that orient themselves to a smaller audience, or position themselves in a hostile relationship to their audience, or embrace univocal, strict, school-based, or difficult styles.

The kinds of aesthetic compromise modeled by writers like Wallace or anthologies like *American Hybrid*, this line of thinking goes, are pro-democratic artistic models. Avant-gardism is antidemocratic. This belief has stood unchallenged to the point of seeming like common sense.

But such a notion rests on a belief in the existence of a general audience, one that can be reached better through aesthetic compromise than through aesthetic radicalism.

In an article for an issue of the *Review of Contemporary Fiction* edited by Wallace on fiction's prospects at the turn of the millennium, his longtime friend Jonathan Franzen gives us what might be the clearest articulation of who that general audience is often imagined to be.

"For much of this century," Franzen writes, "the United States had a robust national literature whose audience could with only slight exaggeration be called a general one." But beginning in the 1990s, he notes, one sees the rise of "the new tribalism—gay, lesbian, African-American, Asian-American, and Latino writers." Franzen allows that such writers are "a refreshing change," but he sees in the decline of the "general audience" a move away from the old project of literary fiction, fiction that has as its ambition an account of "the whole battery of stuff like honesty and responsibility and love and significance that constitutes 'humane values.'"

Implicitly, Franzen draws a line between what he sees as writing that represents "tribal" positions and that which addresses a "general audience" that would be interested in the big questions of humanity. And he maintains that distinction despite the fact that he recognizes at one point in the essay that it's likely that "the 'general' audience our national literature once possessed was always predominantly female" and that "sometime around 1973 women finally got tired of getting their news of the world via (frequently misogynist) male perspectives, and that was the end of the 'general' audience."

In her decision not to read *Infinite Jest*, Hungerford is a perfect example of the kind of female "general audience" member Franzen fears.

For Franzen, however, the end of the (even fake, even coercive, even patriarchally constructed) "general audience" means that literary fiction has lost its motor. So the only answer, he argues, is to "retrench." To "write of nature and the human heart." To accept that sometimes "the truly subversive literature is in some measure conservative."

Wallace, who spends his introduction to the *Review of Contemporary Fiction* issue talking about how the arguments of each of the issue's manifestos on the future of fiction are overblown and flawed, includes a footnote where he quietly affirms Franzen's argument, writing that "Jon Franzen's [essay is] very, very close to being right." But neither Franzen nor Wallace considers the possibility that fiction might benefit from the destruction of the notion of consensus and homogeneity that underlies the concept of the general audience; that the last thing literature should do in the face of a threat to its relevance is to *retrench* into a falsely constructed notion of universal humanity.

If one believes that democracy thrives on compromise, then work that tries to provide an aesthetic common ground might be read as a last-ditch effort to produce a literary culture that can appeal to readers across political, personal, and social divides. Such a culture, one could imagine, would require the abandonment of camps, of factions, of hostility between writers and artists. Divisions among writers, this argument goes, serve only to separate essentially like-minded people at a time when unity is necessary. This is the fundamental premise of compromise aesthetics.

But by showing what can be accomplished by the refusal to compromise, the history of the *Little Review* demonstrates that the conclusions of compromise aesthetics are not as self-evident as they may appear. The *Little Review* offers a countermodel, one in which a wide audience is welcomed into a space that is essentially combative, one that is populated by strong positions of many kinds. And while such a space may not embrace liberal values such as rationality or moderation, it's hard to say that a magazine that allows a celebrity anarchist and a midwestern teenager to be in dialogue with each other isn't democratic.

If it is difficult for scholars like Golding to recognize the democratic gestures of the *Little Review*, it may be because liberalism and democracy seem to inevitably go hand in hand. Chantal Mouffe, however, reminds us that this is by no means the case. "There is no necessary relation between these two distinct traditions," she writes. And "there is no way in which they could be perfectly reconciled."

And maybe that means that there is hope for people like Anderson and me, people who are ardent, critical, sometimes too intense. I used to believe that both democracy and social relationships required an attitude of moderation, of being nice. But I am beginning to wonder what other forms of solidarity and collectivity are available to those of us who value the communication of strong feelings over measured, rational debate. Are we doomed to loneliness in a liberal society? Perhaps. But there might be room for us in a democratic society yet.

5

THE MISSOURI COMPROMISE

I live in Missouri, a state established under the sign of compromise.

Brought into existence with the Missouri Compromise of 1820, the state, it seems, was doomed to a future of liminality and vacillation. Both a slave-trading hub and an abolitionist stronghold in the ante-bellum period, Missouri was a Union-occupied slave state during the Civil War, with armies fighting for both sides struggling within its borders.

Throughout the twentieth century, Missouri was known as a bellwether state, swinging in each presidential election with the political mood of the nation.

The northernmost southern state or the southernmost northern state, Missouri sways from icy-Chicago to balmy-Arkansas, sometimes plunging or climbing fifty degrees in a single day.

Missouri has two major cities, each with one foot in a neighboring state: Kansas City, which faces west to Kansas and the plains, and St. Louis, which faces east, across the Mississippi River, to Illinois.

In the 1960s, St. Louis was not southern enough for Jim Crow laws and landmark civil rights actions, but it was also not northern enough for the race riots that erupted in the Rust Belt cities of Chicago, Detroit, Cleveland, and Pittsburgh. Nevertheless, as a consequence of suburbanization, white flight, and aggressive redlining practices, St. Louis became one of the most segregated cities in the United States.

And then, in 2014, the suburbs catch fire. Michael Brown, an unarmed Black man, is murdered by a white police officer.

Ferguson, Missouri, is only twenty minutes from my home. I watch the protests on television, the cat on my lap, the baby asleep upstairs. I am supposed to be preparing for class, but instead I am half watching TV, half reading Carl Schmitt's 1932 political treatise, *The Concept of the Political*. The book lies cracked down the middle at my side, spine pointing upward.

A TitleMax loan storefront explodes in flames. Shattering glass. Sirens. The newscaster ducks behind a car.

Friends tweet about tear gas and gunshots. I follow the tweets, hungry for information, suffused with a feeling that hovers at the crossroads of jealousy and doubt. I tell myself I would be there if it weren't for the baby, and then I remember how I served as my mother's justification for her own depoliticization. *Children exert a conservatizing effect*, she would explain with a weary sigh. It always sounded like a cop-out.

More broken glass. The newscaster looks giddy, poking his head up to watch the TitleMax burn.

The cat purrs immoderately on my lap, a symbol of idle privilege.

Somewhere between bored and overstimulated, I pick up the book again.

Schmitt is explaining that the world is structured by antagonisms. We judge art, he says, based on the antagonism between beauty and uglinesss. We judge morality based on the antagonism between good and evil. But, for Schmitt, "the most intense and extreme antagonism" is the one that defines the domain of the political: the distinction between friends and enemies.

Liberalism, with its emphasis on compromise, is, for Schmitt, the attempt to imagine that the friend/enemy distinction could be reconciled. For that reason, he argues that liberalism is not a type of political belief; it is the attempt to negate politics itself, to create a world without friends and enemies.

I hear sirens, and I'm not sure if they're on the television or outside my house. And although I am relatively new to the state, I ask myself the question that we Missourians have spent the past two hundred years avoiding: *What side are you on?*

When Missouri petitioned to join the Union as a slave state, in 1819, the United States was evenly split among states allowing slavery and states in which slavery was prohibited. Conflict emerged in the Senate over the balance of power among slave and free states. The dispute was intense and divisive, and political figures worried publicly about the possibility of a civil war. Eventually, the two sides were reconciled through an agreement known as the Missouri Compromise of 1820, which allowed Missouri into the Union as a slave state provided that Maine was established as a free state. The balance between free and slave states restored, the country returned to a brief period of peace.

When the compromise was struck, most political figures were relieved. But many, including Thomas Jefferson, remained concerned. The debate over Missouri's statehood, he writes in a letter to John Holmes, "like a fire bell in the night, awakened and filled me with terror. I considered it at once as the knell of the Union." After the compromise, he continues, that bell was "hushed, indeed, for the moment." But, he insists, "this is a reprieve only, not a final sentence."

Jefferson was writing about the Missouri Compromise, but he could have been writing about nearly any compromise struck in the midst of crisis. Paraphrasing Schmitt, Tracy B. Strong writes that liberalism is "a system which rests on compromise; hence all of its solutions are in the end temporary, occasional, never decisive." Strong's argument recalls the fleetingness of the "Tiny Dancer" sing-along. Compromise does not nullify the conflict it temporarily addresses; it does not touch the fundamental structures that have given rise to the division it tries to reconcile. It is, therefore, never anything more than a brief pause in the clanging of a fire bell.

In addition to balancing, for the time being, the number of slave states and the number of free states in the Union, the Missouri Compromise did something else, something that seems as if it would go against the very principle of compromise itself: it drew a line.

According to the agreement, a north-south line was drawn across the lands gained in the Louisiana Purchase at approximately the thirty-sixth parallel, excluding slavery north of the line and permitting slavery south of it. This, too, troubled Jefferson. He writes: "A geographical line, coinciding with a marked principle, moral and political, once conceived and held up to the angry passions of men, will never be obliterated."

Jefferson turned out to be right about that line. The Missouri Compromise momentarily reconciled two opposing positions, but it did so by formalizing a divide between north and south, a divide that had been tacitly emerging but had not yet been formally codified. Once the line was drawn, it seemed inevitable that the nation would divide itself further. And it did. Missouri was established under the sign of compromise, but that compromise did not solve the conflict that necessitated it in the first place. Instead, by making concessions to both sides, it gave both sides power, definition, and tacit support. In so doing, it initiated a process of conflict that would ultimately lead to war.

The block I live on in St. Louis is neither this nor that. Neither densely urban nor suburban; single-family homes march thickly up and down the block mere inches away from one another.

Neither large nor small, the houses are among the few in the neighborhood that are neither imposing four-square brick houses nor tiny brick bungalows. They are uniformly medium-sized. Fifteen hundred square feet. Two or three bedrooms; one or two bathrooms.

Like their larger and smaller cousins, the houses on my block are made of dark red brick. Like nearly every dwelling in the city, they were built to be fireproof under a city ordinance passed after a catastrophic fire in 1849 that required that buildings be constructed out of brick and stone.

Unlike those who live on most blocks in the city, the residents of mine are neither entirely white nor entirely Black. My neighbors are re- tired mechanics and police officers, teachers and musicians, baris- tas and day care providers, military officers and contractors. No one is rich, but most seem to be surviving, paying the mortgage, finding work. In this way, my block is statistically unlike most blocks in the United States today, an outlier in its very middleness.

My block is an outlier in another way too: it is politically neither left nor right. Or, better put, it is vociferously both. By the fall of 2016, the yards begin to visibly polarize. They are dotted with BLACK LIVES MATTER and WE SUPPORT THE POLICE signs. One neighbor flies a rain- bow flag. Another has a bumper sticker of a black-and-white American flag. A blue line crosses the flag at approximately the thirty-sixth parallel.

The bumper sticker, meant to indicate support for the police as the "thin blue line" that stands between crime and law and order, adorns a large, shiny, expensive pickup truck. The truck belongs to the son of a man who lives several houses away from me. An amateur rehabber, he buys up vacant properties to prevent "the wrong kind of neighbor" from moving in. In posts on our neighborhood Facebook group, he refers to the left-leaning residents of our neighborhood as "libtards," posts GIFs of cartoons retching at the mention of gay marriage, warns the neighborhood of deadly riots in advance of the grand jury deci- sion on the prosecution of Darren Wilson, the white police officer who shot and killed Michael Brown. When he is blocked from the group, he pleads free speech.

Think pieces about the problem of political polarization pop up here and there. Blue states and red states. Cities and towns. Centers and peripheries. My block, neither this nor that, seems to offer an opportunity to tear down such divides. But I find myself unable to compromise. I look away when my neighbor approaches. I walk past him without waving. I see his face fall into a scowl when I drive by. We are both aware, I imagine, of the invisible line that separates friends and enemies.

<><><>

Writing in Germany during the golden age of the Weimar Republic, Schmitt develops his concept of the political in response to what he sees as a failure of liberalism. This moment, which saw the institution of the ill-fated League of Nations and imagined that the end of the Great War would lead to the advent of a new age of peace, is one that Schmitt sees as an age of "neutralizations and depoliticizations," of the attempt to erase long-standing oppositions between friends and enemies.

This erasure, he explains, is accomplished by the substitution of two liberal tendencies in place of the political. First, liberalism sees the world as ideally organized according to an economic, rational, instrumental logic. Replacing the political with the economic allows a liberal order to imagine that it could produce a global system based on rational exchange and instrumental compromises.

Second, liberalism relies upon moral and legal reasons for individuals to embrace a social order. One refrains from violence, in this model, not because of a concern for the well-being of a collectivity, but because violence is immoral and illegal; one avoids doing harm not out of a positive love of one's community, but because harming others makes one a bad person. Liberalism therefore depoliticizes by instrumentalizing on the one hand and individualizing on the other.

Schmitt places the arts and intellectualism on the side of individualism, grouping them together with law and morality. I want to tell him that it doesn't have to be that way. I want to tell him that art and thought can be ways to engage with the political; they can be powerful tools for not only understanding but also establishing lines between friends and enemies, and maybe even ways of doing so without those lines leading to war.

But it's too late. Schmitt is dead, after a life during which he rose through the ranks of the Nazi Party. He was one of the Third Reich's most revered judicial experts, justifying political assassinations on the basis of the legitimacy of Hitler's dictatorial power. He wrote pieces advocating for the destruction of any work of thought or art containing ideas influenced by the work of Jewish intellectuals. He presided over book burnings.

Schmitt would have burned this book, the one you are reading, no matter the support it contains for his philosophical arguments. This is because, for him, the distinction between friends and enemies was national, racial, and ethnic. For me, the distinction between friends and enemies is different: it is the line between those who aim to create, profit from, and actively defend unjust forms of structural disempowerment and those who disagree with and challenge those structures.

And, if I'm honest with myself, my sense of who a friend is has an emotional dimension too: it has to do with a feeling of intellectual solidarity that allows me to find allies across time and space. That feeling insulates me against the constant threat of loneliness that stems from my hardness, my feelings of alienation, my tendency to be *too much*.

I feel this solidarity when I read Schmitt's critique of liberalism, and it makes me want to recruit him as a friend. Sometimes I think I feel his hand on my octave. But in reality, he would have eagerly provided legal justification for my murder. Because for him, my Jewishness would have defined our relation. I would be, by birth, his enemy.

<><><>

The Missouri Compromise limited slavery in the growing United States, but it meant that the federal government authorized slavery as well. The line that was drawn across the thirty-sixth parallel defined free territories by means of establishing unfree ones, and by doing so it legitimized slavery even as it sought to moderate it. The Compromise did something compromises always risk doing: it allowed something unjust to not only persist, but flourish.

This wasn't the first time the United States made a compromise about slavery. In fact, most of the significant compromises in early US law existed to avoid confronting slavery, and thus tacitly to allow it.

These compromises have names: The Three-Fifths Compromise. The Slave Trade Compromise. Later, the Missouri Compromise. And, finally, the Compromise of 1850.

These compromises, like all compromises, seem like unique responses to a specific, idiosyncratic state of affairs. It just so happened, we might think, that there were cash crops in the colonies that economically relied upon the existence of slavery. The coincidence of liberalism and slavery was just that: a coincidence.

But there is another way of thinking about this state of affairs, one that would see the slavery compromises less as pragmatic solutions and more as constitutive of the very possibility of the first modern nation founded on liberal principles.

The Italian philosopher Domenico Losurdo contends that liberalism requires the delineation of a "community of the free." The liberal belief in individual freedom works, he argues, only if there is something outside of individual freedom to which it can be compared. One can feel free only if someone else is distinctly unfree.

Liberalism, in theory, meant a universally free humankind. Liberalism in practice meant what politics always means: drawing a line between friends and enemies. In the case of the eighteenth- and nineteenth-century iterations of the liberal state, this meant that "the line of demarcation of the community of the free" was usually racial and ethnic. Liberalism, Losurdo observes, is a political philosophy that espouses values of minority rights, toleration, and compromise, but these values were historically implemented with a glaring exception.

"The paradox we face is this," he writes. "The rise of liberalism and the spread of racial chattel slavery are the product of a twin birth."

And this condition did not stop after emancipation. In *Scenes of Subjection*, Saidiya Hartman argues that in the United States, "the texture of freedom is laden with the vestiges of slavery," such that it becomes impossible to unscramble an idealized liberal set of values from their original manifestation in a system based on slavery. "The long-standing and intimate affiliation of liberty and bondage," Hartman explains, makes it "impossible to envision freedom independent of constraint."

How is it that the most far-reaching, intentionally executed, global deprivation of human freedom coincided with the belief that the state could exist not to limit but to ensure basic human liberty? My education was premised on the tacit argument that this was the product of some kind of mass catastrophic oversight on the part of Europeans and early US citizens.

But thinkers like Losurdo, Hartman, and Schmitt make another possibility visible: if politics always involves drawing lines between friends and enemies, then liberalism, in its effort to deny such divisions on behalf of a shared community of humanity, can end up ushering in a more fundamental divide—that between the human and the inhuman. Structures of exploitation, deprivation, and injustice continue to exist in the United States today, but liberalism cannot account for those conditions. It cannot say, *you are not offered the same opportunities as I am because you are my enemy*, because liberalism denies the existence of friends and enemies. But the reality of structural violence also runs against the story that liberalism tells about itself; it means that each individual is not free and equal.

Faced with this paradox, liberalism disavows and erases. Liberalism says *we*, liberalism says *humankind*, but in doing so it obscures those outside of "the community of the free." The tacit presumption, then, is that those deprived of freedom in a liberal society are not part of the *we*, are not part of what *we* mean when *we* say *human*.

<><><>

My kid corners me in my closet as I am hanging up clothes. *Mama! Thumb war!* she shouts. I pivot and offer my fist.

One, two, three, four, we sing, *I declare a thumb war*. I stiffen my thumb, preparing for battle.

But there is more. *Five, six, seven, eight*, she continues, still wagging her thumb back and forth, *you are good but I am great*. The contest ends quickly. Her tiny thumbs have excellent leverage. She pins me. I lose. Drunk with power, she wants to kill me again. *One more time!* she begs. We start again. And again, she affirms my essential goodness; her essential greatness.

At the time, the ritual makes me smile because it articulates so clearly the relationship between parents and children. Both she and I really do believe that I am good but she is great. But later it occurs to me that the refrain also reflects the strange conundrum of liberal violence. A liberal regime must recognize the full humanity, goodness, and rights of its opponent, but if it engages in violence, it has to insist upon a moral difference stark enough to justify doing that opponent physical harm. It must say *you are good* (because all of humanity is good) *but I am great* (so much greater that my conquest of you serves the larger goals of humanity). Unless, that is, it denies the humanity of its opponent altogether.

<><><>

The political, Schmitt argues, never disappears. There will always be friends and enemies; it is just a matter of how they are defined. For Schmitt, recognizing the existence of friends and enemies in any political situation is preferable to attempting to suppress the reality of the friend/enemy divide, because that suppression creates the possibility for much more far-reaching violence.

The end of *The Concept of the Political* is a terrifying account of what he believed would come of the attempt to replace politics with economics, a reality he saw nascent in the new global orders of his time. And even though I know he was writing in the 1920s, I feel like he is writing right now, at this crisis point of global capitalism.

Under a system of liberal economic imperialism, he argues, "war is condemned but executions, sanctions, punitive expeditions, pacifications, protection of treaties, international police, and measures to assure peace remain." I think about drone strikes. Discrete, covert, and unauthorized military actions. Sanctions and trade blockades that limit civilian access to food, medicine, shelter, clothing. Thousands of migrants dying in the Sonoran Desert and drowning in the Mediterranean. These are what Schmitt ironically calls "essentially peaceful means of force," forms of violence, even killing, that appear to be unwarlike.

A similar form of violence occurred after St. Louis tried to pass a Jim Crow–style law banning African Americans from buying property in certain neighborhoods. The law was ultimately declared unconstitutional. Instead, redlining practices emerged that ensured near-total racial segregation without anything like a visible show of force.

The line drawn by those economic practices still exists: Delmar Boulevard. You can see it on racial demographic maps of the city: 98 percent of the residents north of the line are Black, and 73 percent of the residents south of the line are white. I put my fingers on the line and trace it along the projection screen for my students. I drive that line, looking to one side at boarded-up buildings, and to the other side, only a few blocks south, at Lululemon, Starbucks, an independent bookstore, an artisanal ice cream parlor.

The murder rate per capita north of Delmar Boulevard is among the worst in the country. Someone trained only in political thinking would think that those who live north of Delmar are the enemies of those who live south of the boulevard, and they would wonder what force maintains the division. But no one patrols that line with soldiers or tanks; no territorial map lists it as an official border of any kind.

The segregation that marks the Delmar divide is certainly racial; its origins are in deliberate practices of segregation. But it is also, and perhaps more important today, economic. The median annual salary in the neighborhoods just north of Delmar is $18,000; the median salary in the neighborhoods just south of it is $50,000. Black families who live north of Delmar are increasingly fleeing the area if they can afford to do so. They are moving to suburbs north and west of the city. Suburbs that are historically white. Suburbs like Ferguson.

When economics replaces politics, Schmitt explains, we disavow the very concept of enemies. And yet, we still draw lines. We still constitute one collectivity by excluding others. In this situation, "the adversary," he explains, is "no longer called an enemy but a disturber of the peace." Schmitt doesn't mean a "disturber of the peace" in the way we customarily define it—as someone who bothers people by being momentarily too drunk or too loud. Schmitt means it literally: that the liberal adversary is defined not as a person whose interests run against those of the state, but as a fundamental obstacle to the peaceful functioning of the liberal order.

While one might think it would be better to be a disturber of the peace than an enemy, this is not the case. An enemy is still imagined to be human; a disturber of the peace, on the other hand, Schmitt argues, is "designated to be an outlaw of humanity," someone who has stepped outside the ethical premises that constitute basic human decency and therefore has relinquished the very definition of the human.

Schmitt will never be my friend, but I am enough of a liberal thinker to believe that his intellectual contribution transcends our friend/enemy divide. Or maybe it's less rational than that. The final sentences of *The Concept of the Political* stick to me like a sinking feeling in the gut or a bad earworm.

> A war waged to protect or expand economic power must, with the aid of propaganda, turn into a crusade and into the last war of humanity. . . . This allegedly nonpolitical and apparently even antipolitical system serves existing or newly emerging friend-and-enemy groupings and cannot escape the logic of the political.

Last war of humanity. Cannot escape the logic of the political. These phrases ring through my head as I think about all of the violence, all of the killing, that is perpetrated by the global economic order even if it is never claimed as an act of war, even as no one can define it as a political attack on an enemy.

Schmitt's words sing in the background as I read stories of police shootings, of internment facilities, of child-parent separations, of sprawling refugee camps, of opioid overdoses, of homelessness, of sweatshops, of the rising rate of suicides and other so-called deaths of despair. *This allegedly nonpolitical and even antipolitical system serves existing or newly emerging friend-and-enemy groupings.* And I try to imagine what would happen if it was spelled out for everyone to see, if it was clear that the people dying had been implicitly designated as enemies, or as *outlaw[s] of humanity.* Would things change? Would the friend/enemy divide reappear or be reconfigured? And if so, wouldn't that be the very definition of political change?

6

IN A BOX

It's Super Bowl Sunday 2016, and I'm grouchily pontificating on domestic violence statistics, the relationship between militarism and sports, and the irony of "watching the commercials" as a form of entertainment for overeducated hipsters. Basically, as a critic, I'm engaging in the national pastime of my people: ruining everyone's good time.

(Q: How many feminists does it take to screw in a light bulb?
A: That's not funny.)

Halftime begins. Coldplay does Coldplay's thing. Then Bruno Mars does Bruno Mars's thing. There are American flags. Pyrotechnics. Drums.

And then Beyoncé appears on the screen, and I forget to be jaded and skeptical.

Okay ladies now let's get in formation, she half chants, half sings. Her dancers, in two clean lines behind her, dance in unison, following her lead.

The uniforms of the dancers are clearly meant to evoke the iconic look of the Black Panthers: Afros, black leather jackets, berets. Beyoncé herself is wearing a leather moto jacket adorned with two crossing bandoliers, recalling Michael Jackson's signature style, but also connecting Jackson's legacy to a history of armed resistance.

All of this comes during the first crest of the Black Lives Matter movement, the day after the release of the "Formation" video, with its clear
opposition to police violence. In the video, Beyoncé appears on the
roof of a police cruiser surrounded by floodwaters, evoking the after-
math of Hurricane Katrina. Later, a little boy dances in front of a line
of cops in riot gear. At one point, he raises his arms and the line of
cops raise their hands in the *hands up don't shoot* protest posture. The
words STOP SHOOTING US appear on a wall behind him.

The result of the accumulation of all the antipolice and Black power images associated with the song is that, watching the Super Bowl show, I feel very much like the critic Sarah Mesle, who describes her elation in the midst of the performance. She writes, "There was a moment when my heart stopped, thinking that the world takeover had begun!"

I wonder if literary critics were particularly prone to this feeling. After all, whether implicitly or explicitly, an education in literary criticism has, for the past several decades, involved being taught to be attuned to the ways in which the assertion of aesthetic form—the visibility of artistic shaping that is evident in symmetry, repetition, unity, patterning, and so on—is aligned with the assertion of political power. Caroline Levine summarizes this attunement in her recent book, *Forms*: "It is the work of form to make order," she writes. "And this means that forms are the stuff of politics." Strict forms in particular tend to be associated with the deprivation of freedom. Levine explains:

> According to a long tradition of thinkers, form is disturbing because it imposes powerful controls and containments. . . . In 1674, John Milton justified his use of blank verse as a reclaiming of "ancient liberty" against the "troublesome and modern bondage of rhyming." Avant-garde poet Richard Aldington made a similar claim in 1915: "We do not insist upon 'free-verse' as the only method of writing poetry. We fight for it as for a principle of liberty."

Beyoncé's mandate to *get in formation* stands in opposition to liberty. Both this lyric and the overall choreography of "Formation" suggest a link between aesthetic unity—lining up, coordinated movement, forming shapes—and political unity. And for many critics, Levine points out, "the valuing of aesthetic unity implies a broader desire to regulate and control—to dominate the plurality and heterogeneity of experience."

Levine ultimately claims that formal unity does not always signal an interest in overriding liberty and individual freedom. But it's easy to see how the suggestion that the kind of formal coordination imagined by "Formation"—both lyrically and in its various performances—could be read as illiberal or even intentionally antiliberal, insofar as its militancy and its formal unity run contrary to liberalism's emphasis on individual freedom. Beyoncé's performance, then, could be read as the inception of a revolutionary moment against the hypocrisy of the American liberal experiment, an assault on the foundations of a nation committed to freedom that has, from its inception, perpetrated racial violence in the form of slavery, segregation, and institutional racism.

But there is a problem with this reading, one that Mesle herself points out. Despite her moment of revolutionary hope, she writes of the Super Bowl performance:

> My prevailing sense, however, is one of disappointment. I have seen a certain amount of discussion in the last two days about the final lines of "Formation": "You know you that bitch when you cause all this conversation / Always stay gracious, best revenge is your paper." I feel a little—and this makes me sad to say so please, world, disabuse me of this idea—that with her Super Bowl performance Beyoncé shifted the conversation from her righteous bitchiness to her graciousness, and did so in order to simply make paper, to advertise (as she did immediately after the performance) her "Formation" world tour.

I find it puzzling that Mesle asks for someone to disabuse her of this notion, when it is very clear that Beyoncé is an unapologetic capitalist, someone for whom the accusation of selling out has no meaning because she celebrates her business savvy so vocally. One doesn't need to look very far into "Formation" as a song or as a performance to reach this conclusion: all one needs to do is to listen to the lyric that Beyoncé seems to sing with even stronger conviction during the Super Bowl performance than she does in the recorded version of the song: *I just might be a Black Bill Gates in the making.*

Mesle's concern reveals a tendency to want an on/off switch when it comes to the political significance of art. Is Beyoncé a radical Black performer or a shameless capitalist? If we choose the former, we have to downplay the latter, to see her commercial success as only an incidental by-product of her artistic practice. If we choose the latter, either we have to dismiss the political incitements in her work as superficial or we have to say that all art is contaminated by capitalism and so it doesn't matter that Beyoncé chooses Bill Gates as her aspirational alter ego.

I don't like these choices. I don't like them because underwriting them is the belief that one's aesthetic politics is a moral matter. Beyoncé is an unjustified capitalist (bad) or a secret radical (good) or just making a living like anyone else (good). I don't care whether Beyoncé is a bad person or a good person. I care what her art offers us politically, and, for me, that is not a matter of good or bad; it's a matter of how her work addresses the distribution of power.

It is common knowledge that art, particularly popular art like pop music, is entangled with capitalism. Calling Beyoncé a sellout would be redundant and ridiculous. She makes no secret of the pleasure she takes in her own commodification. For that reason, I wouldn't even think of turning to her work for a critique of capitalism.

But Beyoncé's entrepreneurial ambitions do not entirely nullify the force of the militant tones of "Formation." I think it is possible to read "Formation" as doing two things at once, but on different registers: on one, it openly capitalizes on the total saturation of the market into all forms of life, and on the other, it advocates organized resistance against the violence associated with that reality.

"Formation" can look like an example of the worst aesthetic compromises: it draws from an eclectic stylistic tool kit but it does not imagine itself as part of a unified avant-garde tradition; it gestures toward militancy but unabashedly celebrates capitalism. But the song and performance go against the liberal narrative that often accompanies aesthetic compromises, one that sees the embrace of both stylistic novelty and commodification as demonstrating the irrelevance of militancy today. Instead, the song and its performance use hybrid formal techniques to comment on, experiment with, and even advocate for illiberal forms of militarism: the restriction of freedom, the imposition of force, the violent restructuring of society. We are in danger of missing all of this, however, if we either celebrate Beyoncé's compromises with the market or see them as disqualifying.

<><><>

I give a friend the short version of this argument on our way to the bus out of town, dragging a suitcase with one hand and sloshing a to-go cup of coffee with the other. The conference is over, and we're sleep deprived and punchy from a weekend of nonstop conversation.

But all of the things you think are radical about "Formation"—the militarism, the forcefulness, the structure—that's part of the whole marketing campaign. It's what everyone wants from Beyoncé, she insists. They want her strong. Rigid. Perfect. They want . . . "***Flawless."

"***Flawless." The best-worst Beyoncé song.

Best, because Chimamanda Ngozi Adichie's cameo in the song, in which she describes the premises and goals of feminism in strikingly clear and compelling terms, arguably managed to reinvigorate feminism for a new generation of young women. I saw this happen in the interval between 2012 and 2014. Suddenly women in my classes went from saying that they believed in equality for women but they didn't want to call themselves feminists because *they weren't angry about it* to defining themselves as feminists without hesitation. Noticing this, I finally asked one of them how she came to embrace feminism and she said, without a beat: "****Flawless.*" That's when I first watched the video, right there in the classroom, because I needed to see what sorcery had achieved this conversion.

Worst, because the song's chorus, *I woke up like this . . . flawless*, is meant to be an anthem of self-confidence but, when it is sung by a perfectly made-up Beyoncé, may actually convey the opposite message: if you wake up looking not like Beyoncé, but like a wrinkled, puffy, greasy mess, something is wrong with you.

When I think of "***Flawless," I think of another friend of ours who was also at the conference, and how, before we started talking about Beyoncé, we were marveling at her accomplishments, her poise, the shine that seems to emanate off of her and her work. If there's anyone who I would believe wakes up looking as beautiful and put together as Beyoncé, it's her.

I'm also familiar with the danger of perceived flawlessness. Once, I asked if she ever thought she might take a break and she laughed. When that happened I suddenly understood how my mother must feel when she asks me with concern if I think *things might slow down sometime soon* and I balk and groan and say something like *mom that's not how this works* and she asks if I want her to hang out with my kid so I can take an hour to relax and I say *sure that way I could fit in an extra run* and she nods but gives me a maternal look that I can't look back into because it makes me feel unbearably small.

My friend stops walking for a moment, takes a sip of her coffee, and says *the thing is, she won't be able to do it forever; her body is going to push back against it* and I forget for a minute who it is we're talking about.

Oh, right. Beyoncé. Her form. Her lean, forceful body. Her perfectly controlled movements. Precision. Perfection. Flawlessness.

I wonder: Am I drawn to "Formation" because of the political implications of its form or simply because of its refusal of all things soft?

Is my intellectual critique of compromise merely a justification for my own tough shell?

And finally, in seeing an alternative model for political art in figures like Beyoncé, one that embraces illiberal—albeit imperfect, provisional— forms of refusal, am I simply advocating for an aesthetics of strength?

If Beyoncé's invocation of militancy in "Formation" is merely at the service of a performance of her own stamina, virtuosity, and control, then it can be read as an incitement to work as hard, to be as beautiful, as talented, as the superhuman that is Beyoncé. And whereas at best that cultivates a bad form of celebrity worship, at worst it can start to look like a celebration of the individual over the collective, a desire to give up the power of the people to a single exceptional figure.

I think my friend might be right about Beyoncé in general. She can be a figure of extraordinary strength and beauty, and when she serves that function, the consequences are ambivalent at best. But "Formation," as a song and as a performance, is not simply about a single exceptional individual. *Get in formation* is certainly a command that implies leadership, as someone has to give the order. But the song also invokes the shaping force of something inherited and limiting: the *form* of "Formation."

In the "Formation" Super Bowl performance, that form—the regimented lines and shapes made by Beyoncé and her dancers—can be traced back to a long tradition of historical forms, from eighteenth-century fife-and-drum regiments to the innovations of HBCU show bands, and from the military drills of the Black Panthers to the patterns in which football players array themselves at the line of scrimmage, which are also called "formations." The form therefore brings with it residue and subsequent restrictions from the institutions that shaped it, including both colonial and anticolonial armies, both historically white and historically Black colleges, antiracist organizations and American professional football.

In that way, "Formation" is drawing from a similar logic as a poem by Terrance Hayes, one of the sonnets in his book *American Sonnets for My Past and Future Assassin*. This one is about the form of the sonnet itself. It begins:

> I lock you in an American sonnet that is part prison,
> Part panic closet, a little room in a house set aflame.

Is the sonnet form a prison or a panic closet? Is it a form of captivity or a form of security? Either way, the sonnet is confining, requiring as it does that one submit oneself to the strictures of a historical form. So why would a poet choose the limitations of a sonnet in our historical moment, one in which it is perfectly permissible, if not encouraged, to toss aside inherited forms?

One answer can be found later in the same poem, when Hayes develops an extended metaphor of a crow trapped inside a gym. The pun gym/crow invokes the history of racial violence, but the metaphor extends beyond a simple allegory for segregation, as the crow experiences "a beautiful catharsis trapped one night / In the shadows of the gym," and the gym, a "box of darkness with a bird in its heart," seems to morph into a metaphor for the sonnet form itself by the end of the poem, containing as it does "voltas of acoustics, instinct & metaphor." The history of racial segregation is cast, like the sonnet, as both restrictive and a space for a certain kind of creative invention.

In an interview with *Prairie Schooner*, Hayes was asked, "What interests you about form, and how does it inspire you?" Hayes, who chose to answer all of the interviewer's questions by referencing a set of drawings, replied "D4," indicating the following images:

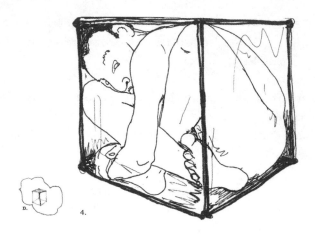

4.

This is a powerful visual comment on the restricting force of form, one that would appear to run in direct opposition to the notion of the exceptional superhuman, the Beyoncé of "***Flawless." The body in this image is forced to conform to a preexisting shape, one that limits its capacities to express itself freely. The drawing doesn't give a ready answer as to why form is interesting or inspiring—if anything, the form of the cube looks like an affliction rather than an opportunity. But that's the point: art made within that form will inevitably carry the mark of limitation and therefore reflect the existence of structures beyond the individual that shape and constrain expression.

Yet form's constraining properties can also afford opportunities for the performance of individual virtuosity. Elsewhere, Hayes has compared writing within set forms and structures to break dancing against yourself, except the formally constrained you is break dancing in a straitjacket. The straitjacketed version of yourself is "automatically going to win," he explains, because "being less free shows us your skill."

"It's just more impressive," he insists.

So working within a historically limited form can also be a means to declare one's exceptionality; to prove one's superiority. The box can be a container, an equalizer, a reminder of social embeddedness. But it can also be a cage that one can, Houdini-like, use to perform one's uniqueness.

Hayes seems to be in this latter category: interested in boxes, but also interested in escaping from them. In an interview at Lit Hub with Jeffrey J. Williams, he describes his work as moving flexibly among a range of poetic movements:

> When I'm at a conference that's full of formalists, they say, "Oh, you're a formalist"; if I'm at an African-American retreat, people say, "Yeah, you're an African-American poet." I'm interested in form; I'm interested in culture. . . . People come up to me saying, "You know, I think of you as a confessional poet." That's OK too; I think the word means to be opened up. . . . I'm interested in Language School poetics, too. . . . I feel like everything's on the table, and I can use it all. I don't necessarily have to commit to one circle, even though I feel people pulling me, "Be on my team, be on my team!" and I'm not sure if I want to be only in your part of the house.

It's easy enough to see why a poet would want to escape the kinds of definitions Hayes describes, particularly since many of these identifications are not and should not be mutually exclusive. But I also think that the belief that one need not identify with a movement is something that reflects an individualist impulse in the culture at large. I am not saying that we need to choose parts of the house, but I do think it's worth examining our motivations for avoiding doing so.

Later in the interview, Williams asks Hayes whether he thinks this aversion to identification with a movement might be generational. "Generation X," Williams hypothesizes, "is more polyglot and less oppositional: they tend toward what one sociologist calls 'the cultural omnivore' and don't have as strict distinctions among kinds of art."

In his response to the question, Hayes seems to think there might be something to this. I do too. Perhaps the most important Generation X incursion into the literary publishing scene of the '90s and early '00s was the journal *Fence*, founded by Rebecca Wolff in 1998. Wolff describes the poetry scene of the '90s as consisting of "pristine blandness" on the one hand "and impenetrable, closed-circuit, dogmatic, programmatic" experimentalism on the other. "Both poles felt like clubs," she writes, "to which I did not belong." She sounds very much like Hayes when she writes in the *Fence* Manifesto, "*Fence* is a resting place for work that we recognize by its singularity, its reluctance to take a seat in any established camp."

Rather than a box, *Fence* wants to offer "a reliable home for the *fence-sitters.*" Given the poetry climate that Wolff describes, I understand the desire for that home. And at its best, the work in *Fence* is like the best of Hayes's work: formally provocative, attuned to the dynamics of language and power, and irreverent toward all orthodoxies, even *Fence*'s own. But I also think it's inevitable that celebrating getting out of all boxes falls into the trap of compromise aesthetics: it will entail a rejection of the kind of militancy associated with movement-based literature, and I wish that wasn't the case. When, later in the *Fence* Manifesto, Wolff writes, "There is nothing radical about this magazine," I can read the statement as oppositional in its way, as rejecting the mandate that one "be radical" according to the existing movement structure at the time, but I also find the strident proclamation of antiradicalism troubling. Reading it from the vantage point of the present, the triumphant rejection of radicalism sounds to me like the kind of impassioned celebration of compromise that allowed for an abdication of politics at the turn of the twenty-first century, the effects of which we are now seeing in the inequality, violence, and democratic erosion of the 2010s and 2020s.

I do agree with Hayes when he objects to having to choose between being read as a *formalist* and being read as an *African-American poet.* This is clearly a false distinction, and yet, for a long time, I, too, believed something along these lines. It wasn't that I thought that non-white poets couldn't be formally innovative, nor did I think that attending to their formal innovations required ignoring their writing about race. But I did assume that form was not in and of itself a matter of race. I believed that form was form, and racial identity, when it appeared in their work, should be read as the content shaped by that form.

I was operating on a false binary. One that, according to the literary scholars Chris Chen and Tim Kreiner, white writers have perpetuated for generations. I thought about race as a matter of content, of *culture*, as Hayes puts it, and dismissed its relationship to aesthetic form. Chen and Kreiner offer an important correction to this belief, pointing out something that should have been obvious, given my interest in the politics of form: "'Race,'" they write, is not "a matter of isolable identities but a hierarchical relation: a form."

We know that race is a hierarchical relation. We identify certain physiological properties (such as skin color) as important because we live in a society in which those properties inform power hierarchies. This is what it means to racialize. Race is also, therefore, structural: it is enforced by social boundaries, by the fact that we invest enormous power in fictional concepts such as *Black* and *white*. It is maintained economically and politically through policies that produce and support racial hierarchies. But none of this has to do with aesthetic form, at least not exclusively.

Form comes in when we consider how these hierarchies are maintained aesthetically, through the production and circulation of images and narratives, sensations and feelings. And while the strong hand of the state is certainly still a significant driver of racialization in the United States, internalized bias, microaggressions, and other more subtle drivers of racism exist as much in the domain of images and narratives as they do in the domain of official policy.

Thinking about race formally makes me think about Hayes's box; about the lonely figure trapped inside. It makes sense that he would want to get out of that box, to prove that he is not defined or limited by it. *But he isn't alone in there*, I find myself thinking. Or rather, he is alone only if the box is understood as personal, if it is his job and his job alone to push against its walls. But if the box is understood as structural, historical, political, then there are others crammed in there with him, their limbs entangled, their arms raised against its sides.

I redraw the cube in my head, imagining that there are many people stuck in that box together. And when I do that, I realize that this new image has a name: solidarity.

I don't think formal solidarity requires adhering to a single aesthetic movement, though movements are often usefully focused on collective visions of form and politics. Movement-based or not, form is most interesting when it is dynamic, plural, and historically complex. And I think form is most interesting politically when it heightens our collective experience of structures of power rather than putting our focus on the specific, the particular, the personal.

Solidarity depends upon seeing the structures that we are contained within. And, in the case of contemporary racism, that can be a difficult task because of the manner in which it is often expressed. When Beyoncé takes as her target police violence, the structures of racial violence are relatively clear. We can see those structures in images: in the line of riot cops; in the confrontation between police and activists. There are also historical formal inheritances from which to draw inspiration: the Black Panthers' counterforce, their highly aestheticized demonstration of militancy against the visible force of police and their guns.

But what about the racism that is expressed in seemingly idiosyncratic moments? How to give form to the racial slight, the tossed-off racist joke, the awkward interaction that momentarily reveals the force of racial history as it underlies the most minute interactions? How to demonstrate that these, too, are structural?

This is the project of Claudia Rankine's book *Citizen: An American Lyric*, a work of experimental poetry that comprises prose vignettes, essays, and lineated verse. The book is, as the scholar Anthony Reed observes, a "somatic archive" of what it feels like to be Black in the United States today. And that feeling includes everything from rage that results from confrontations with clear racial violence, like police shootings, to migraine headaches that spring up from the exhaustion of constantly negotiating one's racial past in the present.

Citizen begins with a section of short prose vignettes. The subject of these vignettes is the pronoun *you*; the stories they tell were gathered by Rankine from her own experience and from experiences of her friends. The *you* is therefore an aggregate *you*; it is, as one of the characters in this section says, not a "self self" but a "historical self," a self that is shaped by an exhausting pileup of racial microaggressions.

You are repeatedly called by the name of a friend's Black housekeeper; *you* are screamed at to get away from a therapist's house while trying to show up for your first appointment; *you* are brought into bitter conversations about diversity hiring and affirmative action by white friends who mistake you for someone sympathetic to their cause; *your* presence in an airplane's "elite" seats is identified as a source of disappointment to a child who does not want to sit next to you.

In a manner consistent with the way microaggressions tend to operate, each of the vignettes taken separately could be of ambiguous status in relation to racism. But unified under a single pronoun, the pileup of these situations becomes a stark testament to the persistence of racism in a moment that is read by some as "postracial," existing, as it does, after the end of legalized segregation, after the election of a Black president. Against this way of thinking, their aggregation insists upon the continued reality of racism by taking what seems to be simply a matter of personal experience and giving it form.

Reed argues that *Citizen* accomplishes this by using the *you* to turn the *I* into "something abstract." Because the *you* is an aggregate, it cannot produce empathy in a conventional sense. It doesn't make you, the reader, feel what I, the speaker of the poem, feel. Instead, it puts all readers into a category, into a box: it renders abstract what might be personal.

The *you* of the microaggressions is a form of abstraction, turning the lyric *I* into something other than a vessel for one person's experience. But I think *Citizen* does even more radical work with abstraction in its second part, which consists of a long essay on tennis star Serena Williams. In the essay, an effort to understand why Williams cannot escape persistent and damaging racialization on the tennis court, Rankine invokes Zora Neale Hurston's famous statement "I feel most colored when I am thrown against a sharp white background." She is interested in what happens to that line when it is reimagined by the visual artist Glenn Ligon.

An image of Ligon's work appears in *Citizen*:

Glenn Ligon, from Untitled (Four Etchings) *(1992)*

For Rankine, the way Hurston's line is repeated in Ligon's work reads like "ad copy for some aspect of life for all black bodies." This is because the artist "used plastic letter stencils, smudging oil sticks, and graphite to transform the words into abstractions." A Black body becomes the abstraction of Blackness. A white background becomes the abstraction of whiteness. The articulation of a phrase becomes a smudge of blackness that, by the bottom of the canvas, has obscured the white background, beginning to recall the annihilating abstraction of Russian avant-gardist Kazimir Malevich's *Black Square*.

Kazimir Malevich, Black Square *(1915)*

It might seem like a stretch to compare Malevich, an early-twentieth-century Russian socialist avant-garde painter, to the late-twentieth- and early-twenty-first-century work of Ligon and Rankine. But Malevich is still with us, insofar as his is one of the foundational theories of abstraction in visual art. As the scholar Boris Groys explains in his work on the Russian avant-garde, the painter ascribed enormous power to artists, believing that they were "capable of controlling, modifying, or harmonizing . . . hidden stimuli," stimuli that, in his opinion, were so powerful and determining that they eclipsed any need for law. Malevich famously declared that there should be "no special rights and liberties for art, religion, or civil life." Artists, those who know "the laws of pure form," are second only to the totalitarian state, which is, much like a work of art, "an apparatus by which the nervous systems of its inhabitants are regulated." Abstraction and *pure form*, for Malevich, are therefore illiberal, affective, and political.

Malevich's illiberalism is not Rankine's illiberalism. When, in 2015, a racist joke was found scrawled in charcoal beneath the black paint of *Black Square*, the resonances between works like Ligon's and Malevich's became only more complex. But I think *Citizen* does demonstrate interest in the "hidden stimuli" of internalized racism, and it does marshal abstract form in an effort to control and modify those hidden stimuli in a manner that resembles Malevich's most radical illiberal hopes for abstraction. Consider, for instance, the most famous poem in *Citizen*, an almost-haiku that reads:

> because white men can't
> police their imagination
> black men are dying

This symmetrical poem, with its five syllables / eight syllables / five syllables structure, positions white men and Black men on opposite sides of a line that separates them, a line that reads "police their imagination." *Polic[ing] their imagination* is put forward as the failure of white men; the failure that causes the deaths of Black men. Black men die because white men can't police their own imaginations. And, to emphasize this point, the page facing the haiku consists of a list of names of Black people killed by white people, a list that grows longer with each subsequent printing of *Citizen*.

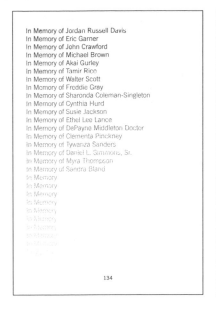

Is it a stretch to think that the poem might be saying something about the aspirations of *Citizen* as a work of literature? If white men can't police their own imaginations, who will? Is this the role of art? Of form? If abstraction has, since Malevich, been imagined to have as its power a kind of control, is *Citizen* offering itself up as a counterform, a counter-policing, a work of art that can go beyond the liberal appeal to the individual and attempt a refiguring of the very form of race itself?

Just as Beyoncé's Super Bowl performance did not lead to a world take-over, even the enormous success of *Citizen* did not thoroughly refigure the imaginations of white people in the United States. It will take more than art to end racism. But *Citizen* and similar works likely have accomplished political work, priming the public for large-scale protests such as those that followed the deaths of Freddie Gray, Sandra Bland, Alton Sterling, Philando Castile, and George Floyd.

Can a heightened presence of form in art foreground the existence of social structures like race? If so, art made in that mode would be an experiment with how the material of oppression can be both formally felt and also struggled against collectively; it would show us both the box and the figures stuck inside, pushing against its walls.

Race is one of the boxes that can function this way; there are many others. But the point is that the formal limitation is not there only as a form of entertainment, as a challenging obstacle. It is there as a figure for structural oppression, something that it takes more than one exceptional individual to overcome.

In her essay on Beyoncé's *Lemonade*, Emily Lordi has an account of how race, gender, and form coincide in the genre of soul. Lordi observes that the album brings together a staggering number of Black female voices, from historical figures to backup singers and songwriters, many of whose achievements have been ignored or erased. But the album does not merely acknowledge the existence of these women and their labor. Instead, Lordi tells us, through sampling, lyrical references, and arrangement, it "constructs a quiet army" of women "who have worked too hard for the money, or whatever else they could get, and are not forgetting." This tribute to hard work and suffering, she argues, is at the core of soul music as a genre and it is what makes Beyoncé's stylistically eclectic work recognizable as falling within the soul tradition.

For Lordi, the collective articulation of shared suffering and persistence over time is what the genre of soul music does, again and again, on the level of form. This articulation is, crucially, the flip side of the exceptional individual. The exceptional individual hides the hard work that underpins her success; soul showcases that work. The exceptional individual appears uniquely capable; soul demonstrates that struggle is collective. The exceptional individual is alone onstage; soul highlights backing vocalists, dancers, collaborators of all kinds.

In our historical moment, one that celebrates individuals precisely to the degree to which they are understood to be able to lift themselves out of their collective contexts and demonstrate their exceptionality, soul's exposure of shared work, of vulnerability and struggle, of exhaustion and even defeat, seems to me to be particularly valuable.

Abstraction and symmetry; soul and the sonnet; the police line, the line of dancers, the three-line haiku: these forms do something other than affirm the exceptional individual. They invoke collective power, the power of history, of structure, of force. And in that invocation, I like to think that they can tickle something in our brains and in our bodies, something that might make us think, for a moment, that the world could be otherwise, if we can recognize our shared encumbrances and fight those structures with all of our collective strength.

7

BAD PEOPLE

In a contribution to a recent *This American Life* radio podcast episode, producer Elna Baker chronicles her experience using phentermine, a diet pill, to lose 110 pounds and become the person she calls "New Elna."

Old Elna was overweight; New Elna is thin. Old Elna couldn't find a boyfriend; New Elna is kissed sixteen times in eight weeks. Old Elna couldn't find a job; New Elna is hired as soon as she hits the normal BMI range. Old Elna was a good person; New Elna learns a startling lesson:

New Elna didn't have to be a good person. I just had to be thin.

New Elna is unnerved by this, by the fact that, as she puts it, *it's such an unbalanced reward system. It took so much more kindness, hard work, and ingenuity to be a person in the world when I was fat. All this took—* finding meaningful work, social acceptance, and love—*was not eating.* It's a devastating conclusion, but luckily this is *This American Life*, which means there will be a comforting resolution. I can hear it coming even before the music begins to swell at the end of the episode: Baker will come to grips with the existence of social inequality. She will find it disturbing, but she will also understand it. She'll see her place in it. And perhaps she'll commit herself to trying to change the worst aspects of it. The radio piece will be offered up to listeners as a way of getting into the head of someone who knows something about the complexities of this situation, and listeners will walk away feeling like they understand something about people—fat people and thin people—and the way the world does and should work.

Thank god for *This American Life*, the ultimate liberal salve.

It's not the story we're told, Baker says, in a slow concluding cadence, *it's not the one I wanted to believe. But it's a story I can live with.*

More music.

But the piece doesn't stop there. There is a pause. And then:

Here's something I never tell people, she says, almost like a guilty after-thought. *I still take phentermine.* Her friends and colleagues believe she is an insomniac, when in truth *I am awake because I am on speed. And I am on speed because I need to stay thin. I need to stay thin so I can get what I want.*

I know exactly how messed up it is, she continues. *But I also feel like I can't be honest with you, like we won't really get anywhere unless I admit it. . . . I know that all of this is wrong. I don't like what I am. But I've ac-cepted it as part of the deal.*

I listen to a lot of podcasts. I listen to them while I'm walking my dog, jogging, and driving. I listen to them while I'm sewing, cooking, and knitting. I find myself turning to them when I am overwhelmed and don't want to face the thing that is making me nervous. In fact, I now use the number of podcasts I listen to per day as a kind of meta-analysis of my anxiety levels. I turn to them because I know their form.

They are calming, like all set forms: Meditation rituals. Ashtanga Primary Series. Starbucks.

Baker's story stuck with me, and I think I know why. It does some-thing that few narratives do: it gives an account of what it feels like to be a bad person.

I'm not saying that Baker herself is a bad person in any exceptional way. I don't think her piece is suggesting that either. It's more a matter of where the emphasis is put, what image of humanity the narrative leaves us with. Are we all flawed individuals who nevertheless have some core of goodness that makes us recognizable to one another, as *This American Life* pieces often suggest? Or are we trying our best in a flawed system that makes us doomed to perpetuate injustice, to be, in some respects, bad people? Baker's story falls in line with the latter view. Taking phentermine in order to ensure that she is never again doomed to be Old (Nice) Elna isn't an exceptionally bad thing to do, but the eeriness of the end of the piece is in its concession to the badness that structures contemporary life, in its insistence that most of us won't get out, won't challenge the status quo, will inevitably take the opportunities given to us even if they are unjust, even if they are bad for us and for the people around us.

Stories of being bad people show us what compromise means for people with access to privilege. They tell us that we will, with very few exceptions, accept the deal.

There are bad people like Frank Underwood in *House of Cards*, Satan in *Paradise Lost*, and Hannibal Lecter in *Silence of the Lambs*. These are charismatic villains, bad people who revel in their badness. Then there are the hapless bad people, one-time good people who ultimately ascend to villainous heights, like Anakin Skywalker in the *Star Wars* films. And, of course, there are the antiheroes who have become staples of prestige television: Walter White of *Breaking Bad*; Tony Soprano of *The Sopranos*; Kendall Roy of *Succession*. But the bad people who fascinate me aren't villains, nor are they heroic, even in the ambivalent mode of the antihero. They are vortexes of identification. These are figures that are bad, but in a mundane, almost accidental way.

I'm thinking of bad people like Piper Chapman on the television series *Orange Is the New Black*. From its inception, the show uses comically privileged Piper as a way into the US criminal justice system, a system that disproportionately affects people who are not as white as she is, not as rich as she is, or both. "Piper was my Trojan Horse," Jenji Kohan, the show's creator, explained in an interview with NPR's Terry Gross at the time of the show's launch, in 2013. "You're not going to go into a network and sell a show on really fascinating tales of Black women, and Latina women, and old women and criminals. But if you take this white girl, this sort of fish out of water, and you follow her in, you can then expand your world and tell all those other stories."

Piper is not just, as Kohan puts it, "the girl next door, the cool blonde." She is also politically similar to the intended mostly white, mostly liberal audience of the show: naive enough to be surprised by the overt racial segregation at the prison and left-leaning enough to find it distasteful. Over time, however, Piper learns how to work within the prison system, which includes exploiting its racialization. This comes to a head in season four, in which Piper, coming into conflict with a group of Latina inmates whom she has exploited in a business venture involving the sale of used panties, ends up half-accidentally becoming a white power leader.

The metaphor for the relationship between race and economic inequality is pretty on the nose. A business owner in her life prior to incarceration, Piper simply replicates her position within the prison. The result there, as in life, is the production of economic inequality. Piper gets rich, while her workers earn a much lower wage. But then her position in the market is challenged by Maria Ruiz, an inmate who, along with a group of other Dominican workers, decides to begin her own panty business. Piper responds to this competition by falling back on a more direct method of maintaining her privilege: she engages in overt, violent racism. She asks prison leadership for permission to start a security group with the aim of sabotaging Maria's business and finds, to her dismay, that the other inmates who join the group are white supremacists. Undeterred, however, she takes advantage of the prison's policy of racial profiling and plants a pair of stolen panties in Maria's cell knowing that non-white inmates are regularly exposed to random searches. The panties are found, and Maria gets years added to her sentence.

This sets up one of the most striking scenes of the series: in the middle of the night, Maria's group takes Piper to the kitchen, where they hold her over a burning stove and forcibly brand her arm with a swastika.

She is marked as a bad person.

If Piper is a way into a world of *Black women, and Latina women, and old women and criminals* for white liberal viewers, then at this moment those viewers have no choice but to see themselves reflected in Piper's screaming face during this moment of retribution. At the same time, they cannot deny that the swastika is an appropriate sign for Piper's position. We can imagine Piper responding to the accusation of exploitation and racism in terms similar to Baker's: *I know that all of this is wrong. I don't like what I am. But I've accepted it as part of the deal.*

Karl Ove Knausgaard's six-volume work of autofiction, *My Struggle*, is a 3,600-page chronicle of what it is like to be a bad person. Its title (*Min Kamp* in the original Norwegian) is an intentional riff on Hitler's *Mein Kampf*, a book that itself continues to be an object of curiosity precisely for this reason: We want to know how a bad person is made. We want the vile details. The villainous schemes. The exceptional mind of a truly evil man.

The answer Knausgaard's work gives, however, is disappointing. As it turns out, being a bad person is boring. It involves run-of-the-mill ignorance. Everyday instances of gross and unnecessary consumption. Instincts toward dehumanization that have become banal and almost entirely automatic.

While critics have objected to the xenophobic and sexist comments made by *My Struggle*'s narrator and Knausgaard's alter ego, Karl Ove, I think they exist in the book to support the point made by the use of the title *Min Kamp* in the first place: that this is an autobiographical account of a bad person. Or, put another way, believing that Knausgaard is espousing xenophobia and sexism because of the things his narrator, Karl Ove, thinks and says is to make the classic error of mistaking the narrator of a book for its author. We can look to books like Vladimir Nabokov's *Lolita*, another chronicle of a bad person, to see how just because Karl Ove is the protagonist of *My Struggle* doesn't mean we are supposed to like him or agree with him.

I think *My Struggle* is ultimately like *Orange Is the New Black* in that readers are meant to identify with Karl Ove, but not to emulate him. Karl Ove is so relatable that readers of *My Struggle* have to do something very uncomfortable: they have to confront what to do with that identification.

Knausgaard is adept at producing these uncomfortable confrontations, and not just in his fiction. For example, in a lengthy interview, the critic James Wood asks Knausgaard to respond to criticisms made about his representations of women in *My Struggle*. This is his response:

> Knausgaard: Every time I see a woman, I think, How would it be to have sex with her? I think that's the first thought for every man. Don't you think that? I mean, if you are absolutely honest?

> Wood: I didn't write the book. I don't have to answer the questions.

Knausgaard does nothing to defend himself in this moment. Instead, he exposes his badness as a model for the badness of most (presumably cisgendered, straight) men. As a result, Wood suddenly finds himself confronting a situation in which he has to avoid implicating himself in his interviewee's sexism, which is nothing more, Knausgaard suggests, than the sexism that we all swim in.

Wood's response—*I didn't write the book*—on the other hand, suggests that he wants to draw a line between bad people (presumably Knausgaard) and himself. He clarifies the order of authority, reminding Knausgaard that this isn't a conversation; it's an interview. And in an interview it is always clear who is asking the questions and who is answering them.

That is, unless you happen to be a female senator interviewing a belligerent male Supreme Court nominee, in which case all bets are off.

You remember this exchange. Christine Blasey Ford has accused Supreme Court nominee Brett Kavanaugh of sexually assaulting her as a teenager. There is an excruciating day of testimony, during which Ford gives a painful account of the assault. But then it is Kavanaugh's turn to testify, and the day's proceedings suddenly swerve from the question of Kavanaugh's guilt to the question of Kavanaugh's victimhood, the damage that was being done to him by making him answer the Senate's questions.

It is at this pivot point that Senator Amy Klobuchar asks Kavanaugh if he's ever blacked out from drinking. Kavanaugh responds like this:

> Kavanaugh: It's—you're asking about, you know, blackout. I don't
>   know. Have you?
> Klobuchar: Could you answer the question, Judge? I just—so you—
>   that's not happened. Is that your answer?
> Kavanaugh: Yeah, and I'm curious if you have.
> Klobuchar: I have no drinking problem, Judge.

While I was watching the hearings, I was naively convinced that this would be Kavanaugh's disqualifying moment; that the attempt to override Klobuchar's authority would read to everyone as it did to me: as a desperate act proving the guilt of the interviewee. But the result was the opposite. Kavanaugh's response felt like a vindication for so many men who *don't want to answer the question*, who don't want to have access to their domination.

I didn't write the book, Wood protested. And that's true in the strict sense. But Knausgaard wasn't asking Wood to fess up to something in the book. He was asking Wood to fess up to his culpability in a tendency to see women as objects, one that the bad person at the heart of *My Struggle*, the author seems to say, is merely exposing as the prevailing reality.

<><><>

Exploring the mechanisms and consequences of our own domination is something that most people don't want to do. And yet most of us are, in some respect, participants in systems of exploitation and oppression. This is the underside of intersectionality: most of us are privileged in at least one, if not many, overlapping ways. And yet the tendency is to diminish these aspects of our lives because agents of oppression, even unintentional ones, are bad, and the last thing anyone wants to be is a bad person.

One way to understand the incredible force of Kavanaugh's adolescent outbursts is to see them as a galvanizing performance of how privileged subjects refuse to engage with their domination. What happens if you are called on to account for your violence? The success of the Kavanaugh testimony suggests an answer: demonstrate that the process is a hell no one should have to endure. That is why the most important moment in the Kavanaugh hearing was Lindsey Graham's pronouncement of Kavanaugh's victimhood:

> Graham: Would you say you've been through hell?
> Kavanaugh: I've been through hell and then some.
> Graham: This is not a job interview.
> Kavanaugh: Yeah.
> Graham: This is hell.

Karl Ove agrees. Here he is on being taken to task for his damaging representation of his father's family: "It feels like I've gone to hell. I can't explain it. It's just hell."

Usually this feeling of being in hell makes people deny their actions. Or refuse to answer questions. Or bite back. But this is a missed opportunity. Being afraid of being exposed as bad people can paradoxically make it harder to acknowledge the structures that create badness in the first place. Confronted by the exploitative logic of capitalism, it's easier to say *I'm just trying to make a living* than to say *I feel terrible that I am benefiting from an exploitative system, but I don't know how to challenge it*. Stuck in jobs, industries, and institutions with unjust policies, it's tempting to say *I don't make the rules*.

The other option seems to be to try, against all odds, to be good. There are powerful social incentives to display, like so many peacock feathers, good opinions, good things, a lifestyle of organics and charity; of bumper stickers and cloth diapers. The fear of being bad can lead to a desperate search for purity, imagining that it is possible to be good enough to escape the terrifying fate of being exposed as a bad person. But doing so perpetuates the myth that bad systems are changed by the individual behavior of good people.

This is how political questions get turned into moral ones, making the remedy for deep and enduring systems of injustice a matter of sorting out good people and bad people. But moralizing politics in this way risks producing situations like the Kavanaugh hearings, situations in which people get so tired of trying to be good that they vociferously justify their badness. This is one way to read the appeal of neofascist groups such as the Proud Boys, who boastfully identify as "male chauvinists." The fear of being exposed as a bad person is exhausting. After a while, it makes sense that some people would say, *yes, I am bad. And look how very bad I can be.*

Since bad structures make for bad people, the only remedy for this is structural change. But in the meantime, I think there is value to the directness and honesty that Baker displays in her admission at the end of her *This American Life* piece. If it is increasingly difficult to avoid being a bad person, one role for art might be to find innovative ways to foreground that fact. I think Baker's piece, *Orange Is the New Black*, and *My Struggle* do this. These works suggest that the effort to be good is less important than the clear-eyed recognition of how so many of us are doomed to be bad. Because it is that recognition—that bad people are structural symptoms, not outcomes, of a societal focus on individual morality—that is the first step toward meaningful change.

8

SELLING OUT

It was 1992 and I was thirteen years old. Throngs of popular girls at my middle school had begun wearing Nirvana T-shirts and Doc Martens. These were the girls who had sent me running to the basement stairwell to eat my lunch every day a year earlier because I wore Nirvana T-shirts and Doc Martens. And now they looked just like me. Except, of course, they were prettier. And, worse, they didn't see any dissonance between being popular girls—cheerleading, mean-girling, et cetera—and their newfound look. The music I loved, with all of its apparent oppositional force, with its boys in dresses and girls in boy jeans; with its *i'm so ugly that's ok cause so are you*; with its screeds against conformity and superficiality; all of this had become appropriated by all of the things it was presumably against.

Enraged, I glued together a profoundly unsubtle collage of images of runway models in flannel shirts and military tanks in combat. At my local Kinko's copy shop, I made fifty eleven-by-seventeen copies of the collage, running them through the machine twice: first on the black ink setting and then on the red ink setting. When they were done, the red and the black versions of the images were just a tiny bit askew, so that the red and the black vibrated against each other angrily. On top of the images I copied a square of text, printed on my parents' dot-matrix printer, that outlined in all caps the demand that POSERS LEAVE OUR YOUTH MOVEMENT ALONE. I stapled the posters to every telephone pole on the major shopping thoroughfare in my neighborhood.

At the time, I was totally unaware of my hypocrisy. What I referred to reverentially as *our youth movement* was basically punk sold out, punk made palatable to thirteen-year-old girls like me. I was calling out sellouts in defense of sellouts. The first Nirvana album I heard, the multiplatinum-selling *Nevermind*, had been released on a subsidiary of Geffen Records; I was introduced to them on MTV. My favorite T-shirt, with the phrase CORPORATE ROCK WHORES on the back, was purchased at Tower Records. And even the bands that I first encountered on cassettes at the local music store—bands like Mudhoney and Babes in Toyland—had by that time all signed major-label contracts too. Sure, there were the holdouts, the no-sellout indie-label-forever bands like Fugazi and Bikini Kill, but they were in the minority. All of this began to dawn on me, cringefully, two days later, when it became apparent not only that my posters had failed to begin an uprising against fake grunge fans, but also that most of them had been torn down or covered up, intentionally, it seemed, based on the perfect overlap of the new posters on mine, with flyers for upcoming all-ages shows.

Clumsy as my attempt to call out sellouts was, any version of this project was doomed from the start. I was unknowingly caught in a paradox that was particularly acute in the 1990s. This was a decade in which, according to the editors of the *Baffler*, "the more closely American speech was brought under centralized corporate control, the more strenuously did our advertising, TV sitcoms, and even our management literature insist on the virtue and widespread availability of revolution." As media corporations consolidated, advertising increasingly took on a pseudo-countercultural stance. "In economic terms," the editors explain, "the nineties were years of unprecedented consolidation; in terms of official culture, they were years of unprecedented radical-talk."

With corporate-sponsored entities increasingly championing radicalism, it is easy enough to see how a kid like me could get confused and think she was protecting a revolution, when in fact she was protecting an advertising campaign.

Some twenty-odd years later, Stephanie Burt would refer to one of my essays on compromise aesthetics as espousing "no-sellouts agendas."

She would argue that such a position is "a road to an aesthetic—and a political—dead end."

My first response was indignation: *That's a total misunderstanding*, I insisted to myself, to my friends, to anyone who would listen. *I don't have a "no-sellouts agenda."*

But secretly I think that Burt might be right, that there might be something of that thirteen-year-old left in me. And if that's true and if she's still there, as for the *aesthetic and political dead end* part: I couldn't agree more.

"Sclerotic and decrepit, most contemporary academic work about late twentieth-century art is based on a doddering scaffold of outmoded thought," argues Johanna Drucker in a provocative attack on the state of art criticism at the dawn of the twenty-first century.

Sclerotic. Decrepit. Doddering. Outmoded. When one hears these words associated with art criticism, one might imagine a gray-haired scholar stooped over his pile of dusty books, penning his latest 150,000-word monograph on a yellowing notepad. His work, one might imagine, is a lengthy examination of a canonical figure, a testament to the Greatness of a Great Man.

But this is not the image Drucker intends to elicit in her readers. The critical attitude that is responsible for the dismal state of art criticism, in her view, is that which is "premised on oppositional models that are the legacy of the avant-garde," produced by "artists and critics [who] cultivate a self-styled radical chic."

The gray-haired man dissolves, replaced by a young woman typing at a Mac laptop in a stark minimalist café in a major American city, writing an essay on a work of art she believes to be a radical challenge to the injustices of contemporary life. She sips a cup of single-origin pour-over coffee; she nibbles on a vegan roasted-pear scone. She is a hypocrite, looking to art as a force of change even as her lifestyle—like that of the artist she praises—relies upon the worst aspects of the system to which she objects.

I know this sclerotic, decrepit figure; I have been this sclerotic, decrepit figure.

This *radical chic*, for Drucker, prevents scholars from registering what she sees as the truly novel achievements of contemporary artworks: their commitment to foregrounding their own complicity with contemporary social, political, and economic conditions. I agree with her here. Contemporary artworks do often foreground their complicity.

But I have enough of an outmoded commitment to critique, to opposition, that I have a hard time swallowing the rest of Drucker's claim, which is that the most interesting contemporary works lay out the terms of their capitulation to unjust social structures without any interest in acting antagonistically toward them.

Drucker demonstrates her argument through a reading of Gregory Crewdson's photographic series "Twilight." Crewdson's photographs, which have been described by curators as explorations into the repressed violence of the suburbs, are large-scale, lush, and carefully staged. Drucker summarizes the prevailing critical view, arguing that most see their pairing of emotional despair and cinematic opulence as "an edgy commentary on our addiction to illusion."

But, she insists, "better to say, a *not* very edgy and a *very consumable* engagement with illusion. Through every feature of production in this work (thematic and technical), Crewdson shows us that he knows the world in which he participates is corrupt." And yet, "his work indicates no qualms, no hesitation, no flickerings of guilt."

This type of art is, according to Drucker, the essence of novelty. It smashes through received orthodoxies. It calls into question the oldest of critical beliefs: the belief that art can be honestly interested in challenging the status quo.

Selling out, in Drucker's hands, is radical. It is the bold refusal of the institutional mandate that art be politically engaged.

But while it may still be daring to be postcritical in the world of art, in daily life it has become common sense. The 2014 Frontline documentary *Generation Like*, argues that, for many millennials, the very notion of selling out is so obscure they don't even have a word for it. When asked to define *selling out*, a focus group of teenagers responds with confusion, one of them tentatively suggesting that it might refer to a concert that has no tickets left. Selling out either means nothing at all, or it means something good: it means that you have successfully marketed and sold your product. That's why Beyoncé can get away with her triumphant *Bill Gates in the making* line: selling out is a mark not of compromise, but of accomplishment. *Generation Like* ultimately makes the argument that this disappearance of the concept of selling out is the consequence of the commodification of everyday life. The same teenagers who don't know what selling out means are those who are encouraged to sell themselves at shockingly young ages to corporations as sponsored Instagram influencers and YouTube celebrities. Everyone, in the economy of influencers, can imagine that they might someday be Beyoncé.

In his book *Kids These Days: Human Capital and the Making of Millennials*, Malcolm Harris, himself a millennial, makes a similar point. But Harris's analysis benefits from being attentive to the material conditions that have determined the generation's course. In a situation in which a changing economy and labor market have made childhood "motivated more by fear of a lousy future than by hope for dignity, security, and leisure time," it shouldn't be surprising that selling out would come to look like a good thing, or, if nothing else, a relief. Millennials do not have the luxury to embrace *not* being economically successful. And this means that we are quickly approaching a moment in which having a *no-sellouts agenda* will not only be naive, not only *doddering*; it will be incomprehensible.

I understand this incomprehensibility, but it worries me. Not because I think it's possible to avoid complicity with the market, not because I don't want artworks to be popular or sell, not because I miss the good old days when critics could make a living off of pointing out how radical everything was, and certainly not because I fault the artists and writers who are so busy surviving that the intentional withdrawal from the business of making money is impossible.

It worries me when complicity becomes not only a state of affairs, but something to tout or celebrate. Because it is one thing to say that we're all complicit, that there has always been an art market and art has always geared itself to that market, and it is another thing to say that we should be done criticizing that fact. That the only thing we can do with the garbage waters of capitalism is bathe in them.

It is one thing, in other words, to note the inescapability of the unjust structures that determine our work; it is another thing to proclaim our peace with them. To do so is the worst kind of compromise.

Perhaps it is this contemporary tension around the concept of selling out that has made so many recent works of fiction deal with the question of their own economic conditions of possibility, their marketing, and their commodification explicitly within their pages. One of the clearest examples of this is Percival Everett's 2001 novel *Erasure*. The protagonist of *Erasure* is an experimental novelist, Thelonious "Monk" Ellison, who is dismayed by the outsize success of a novel entitled

We's Lives in da Ghetto. Monk sees this book as cynical attempt to give the white public a story of Black experience that conforms to their worst stereotypes. Its commercial success only confirms what a literary agent tells Monk: that he could sell more books if he could "settle down to write the true, gritty real stories of Black life."

Enraged, Monk decides to write a parody of a "gritty" Black story, a parody so over-the-top that it will throw into relief how shortsighted the publishing industry is when it comes to its expectations of Black fiction. The result is *My Pafology*, the novel Monk thinks his agent wants, complete with racial stereotypes, bad dialect, and a plot with plagiarized elements from a dizzying number of canonical works of African American fiction. Evidenced by its reproduction in full in the middle of *Erasure, My Pafology* is truly terrible and offensive.

The novel is given a $600,000 advance.

Monk pushes back even harder against the industry, retitling the novel *Fuck* in the belief that no one will be able to market it.

The novel is given a prestigious literary prize.

Erasure confirms everything proponents of compromise aesthetics say about contemporary art. Art is inevitably complicit. But *Erasure* does offer a critique of complicity by giving us the sad version of that story, a story in which writers increasingly find no room to take dissenting positions. In which one can speak to the reality of a political injustice like racism only through the language of the market, and in which the language of the market, in turn, produces further racial stereotypes.

The inevitability of selling out, in this story, does not grant freedom from the orthodoxy of critique. It is, instead, a mechanism of erasure.

<><><>

Or try this one: Ben Lerner's *10:04* begins with a conversation between the narrator, also named Ben, and his agent, who informs him that he will receive a "'strong six-figure' advance" for the novel that the reader already knows will become *10:04*. The story that follows is a familiar tale of the negative consequences of large financial investments in creative endeavors. Ben is emotionally unmoored by the large advance, and he finds himself unable to write the book he was contracted to write.

The crux of the problem appears in a scene in which Ben goes to a fertility clinic to donate sperm to a friend. On the way, he has an imaginary conversation with his not-yet-conceived future child about her origins. She asks about the high cost of the IUI procedure that created her, and then about all of the other costs involved in her birth, her basic life maintenance, her child care and educational needs. And then the imagined future child asks the question that seems to get to the heart not only of *10:04*, but of Lerner's entire career. After tallying the total cost of her life up to age twenty-two and arriving at a mind-boggling figure, she asks, "Is that why you've exchanged a modernist valorization of difficulty as a mode of resistance to the market for the fantasy of coeval readership?"

This question is significant because it is true that Lerner's work once traded in *a modernist valorization of difficulty as a mode of resistance to the market*. Before writing fiction, Lerner published three books of poetry, all of them, in my opinion, brilliant. None of them were what you'd call accessible. And all of them directly addressed the political perils of easily digestible and marketable public language and communication.

The future child's question therefore crystallizes what we know from the very start of the novel: that we are reading the novel that was composed under the mandate of a *'strong six-figure' advance*, that the work of art we are encountering is, at root, something written for money, a compromise between the desire to challenge readerly expectations and the desire to reach a broad contemporary audience, *a coeval readership*. This is the compromise that lies behind most, if not all, contemporary works of literary fiction; it is just rarely thrown at a novel's readers with such insistent force. And yet, unlike most works of literary fiction, *10:04* is interested in how its complicity with the market affects its final form.

The initial plan for the novel, we are told, is that it will expand upon a story that Ben wrote for the *New Yorker*. And the story—the actual story published by Lerner in the magazine—appears in the novel, but only as evidence of the story that the narrator is supposed to adapt into the book. It is unintegrated into the rest of the narrative, awkwardly set into the text in a way that testifies to its unadaptability.

Other previously published pieces by Lerner—including a *Harper's Magazine* essay and a long poem—appear in the novel as well. It is as if this material were cobbled together into a manuscript as much to fulfill a contract as to produce a work of art. The result is that in the end, the novel is not exactly what one might call a "successful" novel, nor is it "a novel that dissolves into a poem," as the narrator imagines in a flight of modernist fancy. It is evidence of a manuscript composed of bits and pieces, diligently delivered to a press that the reader knows has invested such sums of money in it that its publication cannot be taken to be evidence of its quality, but rather evidence of a financial inevitability.

The scholar Jennifer Ashton reads *10:04* as achieving a critique of capitalism by demonstrating what happens to art objects that become commodities. The visible effects of the demands of the publishing industry on the novel are, she writes, "evidence of a kind of damage, of outside forces affecting the work." But, she argues, once this damage becomes part of a work of art, it becomes "something we can look at together," and therefore something we can see critically.

I am drawn in by this argument because I agree that *10:04* has moments of truly compelling political critique, but I also think it's noteworthy that the novel, damaged as it was, garnered such hyperbolic critical acclaim, landing a spot on most major literary publications' best-of-the-year lists and providing the catalyst for Lerner's MacArthur Fellowship in 2015. There was something ironic about this, as the critical success of the book is only further confirmation of *10:04*'s premise: that novels written for money obey the logic of economic investment and return. The press invested money in the novel, and the novel returned on that investment in the form specific to literary fiction: not in dollars, but in prestige.

The reception of *10:04*, the novel's ability to discuss openly the *'strong six-figure' advance* that was its condition of possibility, to describe the damages that advance wrought upon it, and yet to still sell effectively in spite of—or perhaps even because of—that revelation, might mean something much darker. It might mean that, as literary scholar Theodore Martin argues, the novel's self-awareness merely exposes "the distance between the ambivalence it can't escape and the revolutionary politics it sincerely wants but most definitely does not have."

If *Erasure* mourns the consequences of selling out, and *10:04* is more ambivalent, Jennifer Egan's *A Visit from the Goon Squad* verges on an outright defense of selling out in such a way that confirms Drucker's assessment of contemporary art as intentionally, and unproblematically, compromised.

At first, the final chapter of *Goon Squad* appears to be a dystopian critique of a near future in which the mechanisms by which one can sell out have become even more advanced. In this world, even babies have become a target marketing group. Armed with smartphone-like devices that operate solely by hand gestures, "pointers," as the baby consumers are called, start to drive cultural taste.

The surprise effect of this new technology is the belated popularity of Scotty Hausmann, a burned-out 1970s punk-turned-acoustic singer-songwriter, whose music inexplicably appeals to the pointers. Eager to capitalize on this success, concert promoters launch a secret campaign in which social media "parrots" are paid to express enthusiasm about an outdoor concert. The campaign is enormously successful. The scene at the concert looks something like a sci-fi Woodstock, with hundreds of thousands of New Yorkers gathered together by an insidious corporate promotion, dancing blissfully under the watchful eye of surveillance drones.

And yet, as it turns out, this is not a dystopia. The concertgoers are genuinely transported by the songs Scotty sings, songs that are "ripped from the chest of a man you knew just by looking had never had a page or a profile or a handle or a handset, who was part of no one's data, a guy who had lived in the cracks all these years, forgotten and full of rage, in a way that now registered as pure. Untouched." This purity, however, cannot last, not only because of the commercially constructed nature of the concert to begin with, but also because "now that Scotty has entered the realm of myth, everyone wants to own him."

This would seem to be a problem, were it not for the narrator's probing suggestion: "And maybe they should. Doesn't a myth belong to everyone?"

This passage offers a collective utopian vision that is called into being through the mechanisms of selling out. Scotty's individual resistance to being sold becomes everyone's myth because they all *own him*. It imagines a revolutionary multitude convened around commercial art rather than politics, festival chic and baby slings replacing the boots and balaclavas of the black bloc.

But, as the scholar Michael Szalay reminds us, this narrative is also convenient for Egan herself, the writer who "declares her indebtedness to HBO" when she cites *The Sopranos* as a major influence in developing the formal conceit of *Goon Squad*, and then "immediately after winning the Pulitzer Prize, proceeds to sell the rights to her novel to that network." The "closed circuit" between the corporation and art would once, we might imagine, cause readers to be suspicious about the political aesthetics of the novel. And Szalay, for his part, *is* suspicious: "What exactly is being bought and sold here?" he asks.

I am suspicious too. I want very much to refuse to buy what *A Visit from the Goon Squad* is selling.

I say this, but I also know that I love *A Visit from the Goon Squad* specifically because of its most gimmicky, HBO-esque formal techniques: its interlocked characters; its short chapters; its just-right blend of humor and pathos; even its insinuation, in a blatant advertisement for itself, that the shared consumption of popular culture can be a mechanism for new forms of communal experience. I'm a particular sucker for that last one, even if I know it's wrong.

I also love Netflix binge shows, shows like *Orange Is the New Black*, *GLOW*, and *Stranger Things*, even though I know that many of these shows have closed the circuit from art to market to an unprecedented degree, because they are written under the guidance of an algorithm that quantifies audience behavior. The algorithm gives better advice than any agent could, analyzing viewer data to determine what will make audiences watch episode after episode.

In an interview with *GQ*'s Zach Baron, Cary Fukunaga, creator of the Netflix series *Maniac*, describes changing the entire structure of an episode of the show because the algorithm suggested his initial cut would lose viewers. But, Baron probes, what about his reputation as an uncompromising artist, as the force behind challenging films such as his breakout work, *Beasts of No Nation*?

> He rolls his eyes. "I don't think I've ever been able to make something uncompromising. Like, someone commented on *Beasts* . . . *oh, how did it feel to make a movie that's uncompromising?* Like, uncompromising? I had to rewrite my entire third act 'cause we didn't have the money to finish the film. We compromise all over the place."

So it is only an extension of this attitude when he responds flatly to further questions about writing for Netflix: "The algorithm's argument is gonna win at the end of the day."

I find the mechanisms behind this disturbing and my capitulation to it shameful, and yet I count the days to the release of a new season, prepared to do the thing that I know Netflix wants me to do. Bad person that I am, I will sit down on the couch, press Play, and allow the episodes to flow seamlessly into one another.

<><><>

But there is one self-proclaimed sellout novel that still gives me hope.

In one of the final scenes of Paul Beatty's novel *The Sellout*, its narrator describes a comedian who hosts open mic nights at a local doughnut shop. The comedian, like nearly every character in the novel, is an embodiment of a racial stereotype. "Unpaid-electricity-bill dark" and looking "like a crazed bullfrog," he bellows classic your-mama jokes to an all-Black audience.

"This traffic-court jester did more than tell jokes," the narrator explains. "He plucked out your subconscious and beat you silly with it, not until you were unrecognizable, but until you were recognizable." This description of the comedian could just as easily be a description of Beatty, whose novel, like the comedian's jokes, relentlessly trades in racist stereotypes and slurs as forms of unsettling humor.

Beatty's novel, like the comedian's jokes, is invested in turning the unrecognized into something recognizable: its central plot concerns the narrator's commitment to making the de facto segregation of his neighborhood visible by "re-segregating" it. In a project that is more a work of conceptual art than politics, he places signs around his all-Black neighborhood that say NO WHITES. He even makes the neighborhood believe that a fictional all-white school will be built on a vacant lot, a belief that serves only to make visible the fact that the neighbor-hood school has no white students in it in the first place. The problem that the narrator addresses through this project is not segregation it-self, but the unrecognizability of the fact of segregation after its legal prohibition. Simply making the continued reality of racial segregation visible, the novel seems to suggest, is necessary as racism becomes in-creasingly expressed economically, personally, and covertly.

The narrator's segregation project is a matter of labeling things; it is, in that sense, a work of fiction. And Beatty's novel, too, seems to imag-ine for itself this power: through its use of racist language, there is no way for a white reader to enjoy it as a work of Black cultural produc-tion without also self-consciously enjoying the fruits of racism. Beatty imagines himself as selling out—as making racism funny and there-fore consumable—but he does so as an act of subversion.

The comedian also has to deal with the question of a white audience, but he does so differently. One night a white couple comes into the club. "Sometimes," the narrator observes, "they laughed loudly. Sometimes they snickered knowingly like they'd been black all their lives." This goes on until the comic demands that they leave. "This shit ain't for you," he declares. "Now get the fuck out! This is our thing!"

One might think that this is a parable for the white readership of *The Sellout*. It would be easy to read this scene, coming, as it does, at the end of the novel, as condemning any white reader who has laughed along with the book's jokes. *Get the fuck out! This is our thing!* is the ultimate no-sellouts rallying cry. The comedian, it seems, is the voice of integ-rity against the mainstream commercialization of Black culture.

But the narrator qualifies this comparison. "I didn't agree with him when he said, 'Get out. This is our thing,'" the narrator explains. "I wish I'd stood up to the man and asked him a question: 'So what exactly is *our thing*?'"

Throughout the novel, we know that the narrator is the titular sellout in *The Sellout*. His father's friends call him Sellout. He accepts their taunting without contest. But it is only here, in the final scene of the novel, that the designation makes sense.

The narrator is doomed to be a sellout, because unlike nearly every other character in the novel, he does not have an essential concept of what it means to be Black. He can only circulate stereotypes provided for him by the commercialization of his race: minstrel shows, television sitcoms, films, hip-hop culture, and Black celebrities like Condoleezza Rice and Oprah.

And built as it is on these stereotypes, the novel, too, lacks a unified concept of Blackness. But it is paradoxically this lack that allows the novel to convey something much more important: not group identity— not "our thing"—but the damaging structural conditions that create race as a meaningful category in the first place. *The Sellout* might not offer a way out of the system, but it does maintain something that most sellout narratives do not. It insists upon the existence of a clear enemy: the violence of racialization.

"Two things," writes the literary scholar Northrop Frye, "are essential to satire; one is wit or humor . . . the other is an object of attack." *The Sellout* may not offer a way out of the trap of selling out, but in making an object of attack visible, it makes conflict seem possible again.

9

A RIOT OF ONE

Before I am allowed to look at the punk zines and the stickers, the teen memorabilia and the Sharpie-stained notebooks, the archivist has to lock up all of my dangerous things: my pens, my oversize canvas schoolbag, my coat, my paperback. She tells me where to sit. She gives me a foam mat. A single sheet of paper. A pencil. People at other tables gingerly take documents out of manila folders. They place them delicately on their foam mats; they take notes. The archivist brings me my first folder. Inside is a copy of *Sassy* magazine, dated July 1992. I remove the *Sassy* and place it on the foam mat.

I once would have pawed through this *Sassy* with distracted abandon, pulling out pages to tack to my wall, folding the magazine in on upon itself to hold it rigid as I lay in bed on my back. Now the magazine has become part of the historical record. The folder on my table contains a bunch of other mainstream teen and music magazines too. I recognize the covers of *Rolling Stone*, *Seventeen*, and *SPIN* from a pile of magazines I kept in my bedroom. I would sort through them on boring Sundays, looking for images that I could cut out to adorn my school binders and notebooks.

The magazines are here in the archive to preserve the history of Riot Grrrl, a relatively short-lived but important 1990s punk feminist movement started by singer Kathleen Hanna and her band, Bikini Kill. Riot Grrrl bands were female-fronted; their vocals experimented with what a woman's voice could do in the context of punk. Sometimes this meant full-throated singing, sometimes this meant guttural yelling, sometimes high-pitched screaming. And sometimes, in the songs I liked the best, it meant layering a sassy Valley girl lilt over thunderous drums and growling guitars. Riot Grrrls wrote and self-published zines. They met in chapters all over the country. As a teenager, I would see them on the bus, at shows, downtown, and in record stores with their dyed hair and miniskirts and thrifted men's dress shirts and boots and I would wish desperately to be one of them.

The mainstream reporting on Riot Grrrl is thin. Some articles get basic facts wrong. Some sensationalize the movement. Many couch it in clichéd analyses of "grunge" and "alternative" music. The clichés and superficiality of the pieces give the publicity a sense of being belated. The profiles of Riot Grrrls that exist from the early 1990s are only of marginal figures in the movement. Hanna, the movement's putative leader, is nowhere to be found, save in a few reviews of Bikini Kill. There are no interviews. No photographs. The few quotations from her are secondhand.

The bad and incomplete reporting stems from a media blackout Riot Grrrl instituted in 1992. This was a direct response to a few early articles in which they felt betrayed and misrepresented by journalists. Instead, they devoted themselves to autonomy, authenticity, and self-representation. They communicated via leaflets, flyers, zines, and the liner notes of their records. And eventually they started Riot Grrrl Press, a distribution center for the increasingly large number of zines written by Riot Grrrls all over the country.

"The whole point," writes Sara Marcus in her history of the Riot Grrrl movement, "was no compromise."

The rationale for the media blackout was strong. Hanna was a savvy cultural critic; she knew from both experience and her extensive reading in anticapitalist cultural theory that she could not trust corporate media to do anything other than exploit and appropriate a revolutionary movement. So the blackout reflected more than a fear of compromise or selling out. It was a smart political strategy.

The blackout was a highly coordinated and self-consciously revolutionary refusal of the corporate media, and it set clear limits for what the Riot Grrrl was and wasn't. But the blackout was also paradoxically made in the name of a political belief that would seem to run in direct contrast to setting limits: radical pluralism. Hanna and others rejected the corporate media because it was corporate, but even more than that, they worried that univocal representations of the movement in the mainstream press would lead to limited definitions of what Riot Grrrl was or could be. The movement, Hanna and others believed, should be as broad-based and inclusive as possible. Nailing down a single definition, as any mainstream article would certainly want to do, would necessarily be an act of exclusion.

This paradox permeated the entire project of Riot Grrrl. On the one hand, Riot Grrrls wanted total freedom of expression; they wanted the movement to be whatever each individual girl wanted or needed it to be. On the other hand, they wanted to be united, to be more than discrete individuals. As Marcus puts it, they wanted "individual self-expression," but they also wanted "*movementness.*" For Marcus, this was the magic of Riot Grrrl: it gave the movement an ability to mutate and bend. It allowed any girl to claim it as hers. But the tension did cause problems for its organization. As a leader of a movement skeptical of the very notion of leaders, Hanna struggled to negotiate Riot Grrrl's structure.

In one of the early folders in Hanna's archives, I find a pink notebook with RIOT GRRRL TEST PATTERNS written on the cover in bold Sharpied letters. It is undated, but it contains set lists and letters written, in part, during a 1991 Bikini Kill tour. The first handful of pages includes Hanna's big-picture brainstorming about the movement.

Some important questions facing
girl-punks in the 90's....

- † How can we make our scenes
  less white in both numbers +
  ideology?

- • How can we boot support/educate/
  non-punk feminists?

- • How can we draw up a program
  (fluctuating) that encompasses race
  class + gender relations (species too.)
  w/o have any be seen as central
  or MOST PRESSING....ie, for expl-
  iency sake Not doing outreach w/
  punks of color Not including music/
  zines by lesbian punks Not having
  vegan food available at fundraisers
  etc.... THESE ISSUES MUST BE
  INCORPORATED FROM THE BEGINNING,
  anti-racist
  - speciest
  - heterosexist   works (can not be marginal)
  - classist   written MUST BE CENTRAL

Self representation Rules!
   * must est. what is meant
   by RG + the (ind. RG's in
                various tours)

† RG Media Policy #2
   - Will RG even deal w/
   corp. publications/business?
   ie SPIN, elles Rolling St. MTV.

What constitutes an
original band/zine via RG
standards?
   -(idea) Must
   A) Be proformance
      a) few members
      b) few concerned
                cont.
Each one will be
judged separately + discussed
                among

---

† How "collective" will RG
be ???
(idea) The RG Elite fed.
of non square girl punks
will be formed in DC +
Olympia + will be resp. for
all policy decisions + business
transactions (getting shit
                done +/or
allocating shit→ getting
done)
Policy questions/concerns
will be asked of all
girls who rec. RG mailing
a Fazine (RG int'l)
will be comp. to document

---

these question responses
+ dialogues - each
member of RG & FNSPG
will read + talk about
this zine before any
decisions are made.
Unless there is enough
reps among the vegan,
Black, gang, lesbian etc... -
community x10 decision will
be made till ALL PEOPLE
will be considered...

What const. enough.

The notebook's opening page reads:

> Some important questions facing girl-punks in the 90's. . . .
> – How can we make our scenes less white in both numbers +
>   ideology?
> – How can we best support / educate + draw from non-punk
>   feminists? Should we?
> – How can we draw up a program (fluctuating) that encompasses
>   race class + gender relations (species too?) w/out have any be
>   seen as central or MOST PRESSING

Hanna had clear political goals for Riot Grrrl, goals that would not be easy to execute. Making the Riot Grrrl scene less white and generally more intersectional was a tall order given the historical whiteness of punk and the location of the hub of Riot Grrrl in the Pacific Northwest. Even beginning to address these goals would require establishing clear priorities, group-wide practices, and strong senses of who would be considered inside and outside the movement (nonpunk feminists?). And yet, Hanna wanted the movement to be *fluctuating*, to avoid any group or set of concerns to be seen as *central or MOST PRESSING*. Essentially, Hanna was asking how to cultivate a movement that could be intentional while still being as inclusive as possible. She wanted an art movement that could shape without silencing.

These questions become only more acute in later pages in which Hanna begins to think about group organization and policy. Her belief that mass media is to be treated with suspicion ("self representation rules!") immediately leads to a conundrum: "*must est. what is meant by RG + we." If "self representation" is the goal, in other words, then the self—the collective "we"—to be represented has to be defined in some way.

But that definition is difficult if one is committed to a kind of radical democratic pluralism. "How 'collective' will RG be???" Hanna asks. Her answer is surprisingly hierarchical:

(idea) The RG Elite fed. of non square girl punks will be formed in DC + Olympia + will be resp. for all policy decisions + business transactions (getting shit done +/or allocates shit getting done)

In a possible later revision, the word *Elite* is put in parentheses and scratched over with a different pen. A question mark is written above it. On the next page, Hanna uses the acronym RGEFNSPG, presumably standing for Riot Grrrl Elite Federation of Non Square Punk Girls. Here, too, the *E* is scratched through with what appears to be the same pen used to scratch through *Elite* on the previous page.

All this suggests that Hanna eventually thought better of her use of the word *elite* to classify the federation, with all of the hierarchical baggage it contains. But scratching out the *E* in RGEFNSPG isn't enough to solve the problem. The structure she describes—a formation that envisions a governing body advised by a larger group of participants ("all girls who rec. RG mailings")—does have leaders and followers, rule makers and ruled. Whether or not the *E* in RGEFNSPG stands, it remains there in structure if not in name.

Hanna is aware of this tension between the hierarchical structure of the federation and her commitment to inclusion. "Unless there is enough rep. among the vegan, Black, young, lesbian etc . . . community NO decision will be made till ALL PEOPLE will be considered," she writes.

But then, at the bottom of the page, a question. One that has still not been satisfactorily answered. Not by Riot Grrrl, and not by any democratic structure:

What const. enough?

An RG (Elite) fed. of nonsquare punk girls never materialized in the form that Hanna imagined. Riot Grrrl did end up having an elite, but it came in the form of celebrity rather than centralized leadership. The members of Bikini Kill and a handful of other well-known bands, as well as the authors of the most read zines, served as mouthpieces of the movement, whether they wanted to or not. In Hanna's case, celebrity was the cause of substantial ambivalence. Some of her writing indicates a strong desire to lead; in other moments she expresses concern about the strength of her influence or just plain exhaustion.

In her foundational 1972 feminist essay, "The Tyranny of Structurelessness," Jo Freeman observes a similar phenomenon in second-wave feminism's attempt to do away with leadership entirely, an attempt she sees as stemming from the feminist critique of hierarchy. When there are no official spokespeople for a group, Freeman writes, "women of public note are put in the role of spokespeople by default." Freeman calls these women "stars" and writes about the damage that the elevation of such stars can cause to egalitarian movements.

Hanna's position, however, was more complicated than that. She was a star by virtue of her position in Bikini Kill, but she also did imagine for herself, at times, a political leadership role. And the most exciting material in her archive is her writing about her vision for the movement. She vacillated on her perspective on organizational structures and she was deeply ambivalent about her own power. But she never pretended not to have the power she had, nor did she ever get too comfortable with it.

Over the course of five days in the archive, I read through the Riot Grrrl papers in chronological order. It is not, thanks to the media blackout, the story you might think it would be. For the most part, it doesn't follow the trajectory of the 1990s male punk bands from the Pacific Northwest from relative obscurity to overexposure; from underground promise to commodification. Hanna was motivated by a desire to avoid this fate, having been close friends with Nirvana's Kurt Cobain and having seen the way fame destroyed both his art and his life.

The story of Riot Grrrl is not about the perils of compromise, the market, and the depoliticization of the underground. It's a story of a collective vision dissolving into a muddle of passionate voices without direction. The more I read, the more I find myself wondering if the fear of hierarchical power, epitomized in that scratched-out *E*, contributed to a missed opportunity for action.

I wonder this even as I recognize that the whole point of Riot Grrrl was to be antihierarchical, to embrace a do-it-yourself ethos that was motivated both by punk aesthetics in general and by a sophisticated critique of the intersections between capitalism and sexism in particular. So I feel stuck: believing strongly in the accuracy of Riot Grrrl's critique of capitalism and patriarchy, but feeling disappointed in what it looked like in practice, particularly when the revolutionary rejection of hierarchy took the form of liberal individualism.

As early as the second issue of the *Bikini Kill* zine, Hanna's bandmate Tobi Vail expresses concern that "in this environment it is too easy for our doctrines to turn into dogma." She turns to hardcore punk as a cautionary tale. The story of hardcore, she writes, is one in which "an aesthetic that was originally fierce and powerful and in the vein of fucking shit up became the essence of conformity in punk rock."

Out of concern for this hardening of aesthetics, style, and ideology, she encourages her readers to see themselves as individuals rather than members of a group. She writes,

> I encourage girls everywhere to set forth their own revolutionary agendas from their own place in the world, in relation to their own scenes or whatever, rather than to simply think about ours

> This is about making new meanings of what it is to be cool that make real sense to you to do with who you are and what you want in revolution . . . embrace subjectivity as the only reality there

is . . . context is everything . . . an idea of aesthetics as subjective
truth, more on this next time . . . action.

Vail wasn't the only one arguing that Riot Grrrl aesthetics were subjective, that each girl could define revolution for herself. Marcus observes in Riot Grrrl zines a general "insistence on individualism and
multiplicity, on Riot Grrrl as being without any intrinsic meaning or
substance." This, she argues, "says a lot about what they were defining themselves against: namely, definition itself." For Marcus, this was
useful, because the whole point of Riot Grrrl was to smash through received definitions of what it meant to be a girl, definitions that were
enforced quietly, through cultural norms, and loudly, through physical and sexual violence.

But in practice, the result was often simply confusing. There were calls
to action, but little instruction on what to do. There were Riot Grrrl
members across the country, but few directions were given on how to
find them. Some, like Marcus herself, found this enabling: it meant it
was possible to start a Riot Grrrl chapter anywhere, for a girl to seize
upon the general feeling of Riot Grrrl refusal and make it her own. But
for others, the lack of direction was an obstacle. Riot Grrrl could look
like a secret club, sealed off from the worlds of the teenage girls who
most needed the movement.

It would be easy to say that this confusion and lack of access were
the result of the media blackout. Marcus quotes an article published
in *SPIN* magazine that makes this argument. When Hanna refused
to speak with the magazine, the *SPIN* journalists argued that the
singer "gave up the opportunity to reach thousands with her moti-
vating voice." And Jessica Hopper, a Riot Grrrl defector who chose to
break the blackout and speak to the press, argued something similar
in defense of her actions. Marcus summarizes her view: Riot Grrrls,
Hopper believed, "wanted to live safe lives in small underground communities without making the compromises necessary to graduate to
the real world."

But was the problem Riot Grrrl's refusal to compromise? I am not convinced that speaking with the mainstream press was necessary to make Riot Grrrl accessible to more people, and I agree with Hanna that it would have done a lot of damage in the process. The problem, I would argue, was not Riot Grrrl's uncompromising anticorporate stance; it was their residual *you do you* liberalism. It was the notion that inclusivity could best be served by individualism, the implicit belief that liberalism and pluralism were inextricably linked.

<><><>

I remember reading Riot Grrrl zines when I was in eighth grade and feeling desperate to be one of them but having no idea how to join them.

I would write on my hands and arms with black markers, mimicking the Riot Grrrl signature style. I didn't know then that this was an intentional marker of belonging, one that Riot Grrrl developed out of straight-edge punk's trademark X on the hand. It just seemed like something I could do to identify myself as someone who wanted to be part of something.

Marcus explains that when a girl wrote on her hands and arms, it "suggested that one-girl sleeper cells surrounded her at every moment, waiting to be roused." I do remember having this feeling, but it was one not of hope but of desperation. "The problem of female adolescence," Marcus continues, "was so enormous that knowing and naming wasn't always enough to counter it; you needed allies. Write on your hands, and you might find another revolutionary on a bus, at the supermarket, in math class. You had to be ready."

I was ready. I wrote on my hands every day: black hearts and girls with umbrellas and crouched figures under rain clouds. In retrospect it seems like it should have worked. The city I lived in was only a couple of hours from Olympia, the birthplace of Riot Grrrl. I had access to underage clubs, punk shows, streets covered in flyers and band posters. But I was painfully shy and I needed direction. And I only ever saw Riot Grrrls from a distance, always seemingly on their way somewhere else. I remember thinking *where is everyone going?* and wishing I knew so I could go there too.

On my final day in the archive, I am presented with a large box. It is full of letters. They have been opened, but they are not cataloged. They are stacked horizontally in alphabetical order by the last names of their senders. The box ends at *K*. There are two more identical boxes waiting on a pushcart nearby.

The boxes are full of letters that were sent to Riot Grrrl Press, a clearing-house for Riot Grrrl zines, when it was housed at Positive Force, a DC political cooperative that provided space for a variety of leftist groups throughout the 1990s.

The letters are handwritten in black Sharpie or blue ballpoint or multi-colored markers. Some are typewritten. A few are printed out on dot-matrix printers. Lower case *i*'s are dotted with stars and hearts. There are line drawings of girls in miniskirts and combat boots. They come from small towns, suburbs, and big cities. Their authors proclaim their passion for feminism and punk music. They want to be part of what Bikini Kill has called Revolution Girl Style Now. They tell stories of being mocked by their peers, bullied by boys, ignored and berated by friends and strangers. They are ready to take action.

After a while I have to stop reading them because I feel as if I'm reading letters from my thirteen-year-old self, multiplied into a staggering chorus. Were there five hundred letters in that box? A thousand? I crack the lids of the boxes waiting on the cart. More letters. More and more and more.

And then, at the back of the box, I find a single xeroxed master of the response sent to the letters.

"START A FUCKING RIOT," it says, in bold letters on top.

HOW? I plead silently, for a moment thrown back into my awkward thirteen-year-old body.

> find some other interested girls in your school, your neighborhood etc. if you don't know any, make flyers and talk to other girls. i bet

there are some riot grrrls on your very street, even if they don't
know it yet.

Reading this on my foam mat, I find myself fighting back tears. Because
I know, at least for my part, that if any of the things the flyer suggests
had seemed possible to me, I wouldn't have been writing the Riot Grrrls
for advice in the first place.

"DO YOUR OWN THING!" proclaims the flyer, adorned with hearts and
doilies.

My despair turns to frustration. After all, if I, raised in a white, middle-
class, coastal liberal household, felt at a loss as to how to participate in
Riot Grrrl, how would someone without any of those advantages find
access to it?

All of this makes me think back to the Riot Grrrl Elite Federation and
Hanna's concern that it could lead to hierarchical exclusions. She was
probably right about that. But looking at the story of Riot Grrrl from
start to finish, it is also clear that the replacement of hierarchical exclusions with liberal individualism meant that participation became
idiosyncratic and often a matter of whom one already knew, which is
a recipe for homogeneity. The result was a movement that was mostly
white and middle- to upper-middle class. And that was something that
Hanna never wanted.

In her reflections on Riot Grrrl, Mimi Thi Nguyen writes, "I truly believe that riot grrrl was—and is—the best thing that ever happened to
punk." I agree. But I also agree with her when she points out that punk's
"rugged individualism" is part of its white masculinist ideology and that
Riot Grrrl, against all of its intentions, still carried that ideology forth.

For Nguyen, Riot Grrrl rested on "a generalized 'we' that primarily described the condition of mostly white, mostly middle-class women and
girls." I can see that in the overall corpus of Riot Grrrl writing. But the

root of that problem was less the development of a general "we" and more the lack of a specific one. I think this because of Hanna's notebooks, knowing that she desperately wanted an intersectional "we"; that she was willing to imagine a structure like the elite federation to get there.

My sense is that the "we" of Riot Grrrl was mostly white because the participants in Riot Grrrl were mostly white, and each of their individual voices was elevated as an expression of Riot Grrrl identity.

Hanna wanted pluralism. Vail wanted pluralism. They wanted Riot Grrrl to be broadly inclusive, to shut no one out. But based on the history of the movement, it seems that pluralism might have been better achieved by illiberalism than by liberalism; that inclusion might have been better served by limitation, by shape, and by structure, than by the elevation of the individual. I think of Terrance Hayes's cube and the way a recognition of solidarity can emerge out of a feeling of shared restriction, but I don't know what that would have looked like for Riot Grrrl. Punk is, after all, all about smashing through limits; it's about the refusal of authority. Nevertheless, I am convinced that less "do your own thing" could have allowed the movement, paradoxically, to appeal to more people.

While Riot Grrrl is now historical, enshrined in the archive, the danger of assuming that liberalism is a vehicle to pluralism remains, because the alternatives to do-your-own-thing seem to be rigid forms of hierarchy and authority, that shameful *Elite* scratched out in pen. There are, however, alternatives, and these, too, are visible in the Riot Grrrl story. No one told Riot Grrrls to write on their hands, but it became a sign of membership. What if such norms were embraced and codified rather than seen as dangerous indications of creeping conformity? I find punk inspiring because it shows how political art movements can self-consciously cultivate a style by which one can recognize one's friends. And despite the historical problems with punk's masculinism, its whiteness, and its individualism, I'm convinced that it continues to provide an important example of how art, especially in its most illiberal variants, can draw lines and force its audience to publically choose sides. In short, punk is an example of how art can help make politics visible.

10

TRUCKER HATS AND TORCHES

Ayn Rand is not my friend.

Icon of the far right that she is, I vehemently disagree with nearly everything that she stands for: the primacy of competition, the natural-
ness of inequality, the unavoidability of scarcity, her veneration of the
strong, and her moral condemnation of the weak.

So why do I agree with her about compromise?

The compromiser, she writes, is the person "who dispenses justice by
condemning both the robber and the robbed to jail, who solves conflicts by ordering the thinker and the fool to meet each other halfway." She believes that compromise cannot be held up as a value, as
an end in and of itself, because to see compromise as a desirable outcome, as a place to arrive, is a violation of the very concept of justice.
I think so too.

And I have to confess, Rand is not my only would-be enemy with whom
I find myself in strange solidarity when it comes to compromise and
the liberal ideology that supports it. There is Carl Schmitt the Nazi.
There are the anonymous right-wing trolls who comment on my essays online, not to call me out, but to praise my critique of liberal com-
mercialism. And there is Gavin McInnes, leader of the hate group the
Proud Boys and self-styled "white male chauvinist," who is drawn to
the illiberal promise of art just as I am.

I am confronted with the McInnes example by a friend who is writing
a book on the alt-right. I send him a few pages of my book manuscript to

get his thoughts. He sends me a link to a video of McInnes's talk show on the ultraconservative YouTube channel Rebel News.

McInnes's topic for the episode is unity. Responding to a split between neo-Nazis and the rest of the far right, he invokes his own punk rock roots as a remedy.

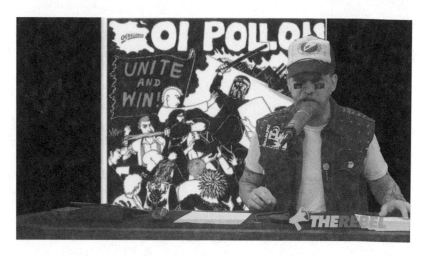

Unite and win! Punx n' skins! he sings off-key, with Oi Polloi growling behind him, before launching into a lecture about how recognizing a shared fundamental belief in the supremacy of Western culture can bring the right together.

Within less than a year of this video's posting, the "Unite the Right" rally will be held in Charlottesville, Virginia. It will begin with a parade of white men carrying torches, shouting, "Blood and soil." And it will end with the murder of Heather Heyer, a thirty-two-year-old anti-racist activist.

My friend's point is that punk's oppositional style, its refusal to compromise, can go both ways. The members of Oi Polloi may have been antifascist anarchists, but the notion of uniting to fight against the system can support the right just as easily as it can the left.

In essence, my friend is asking me to clarify who my friends and enemies are.

"Everyone on the right needs to listen to Operation Ivy!" McInnes declares at the end of the video, as the opening chords to their song
"Unity" swell behind him. Remove "on the right" from his sentence
and you have the exact music-nerd tone with which I schooled my
peers from middle school onward about the bands I liked.

His index finger is raised in a gesture that I recognize. It's the same
gesture I make when I'm overriding someone else's claim. I make
it during casual conversations, at academic conferences, at dinner
parties.

I have recently seen my child make this gesture. She does it while
she's singing along to her favorite song: Phil Ochs's antiwar anthem
"I Ain't Marching Anymore." I love the song too. It's a song of shameless didacticism.

I made that gesture a million times while explaining to my bandmates
why I would not be turning off my distortion pedal. Why our sound
needed a unified style to anchor its oppositionality.

It's a gesture that says *shut up and listen.*

<><><>

There is a question that I am often asked when I talk with friends about this book, the one you are reading. It amounts to this: How can I account for my critique of liberalism when the most vocal groups doing so these days are on the far right?

I am summarizing the question as it would be asked directly, but in practice most people are far more tentative. They talk around the question, slowly circling in on the real point: the possibility that my work might be complicit with white supremacy and fascism. Even just asking the question, it seems, feels dangerous. This is because those who ask it are afraid I will hear the question as an accusation, as the sug- gestion that I might be a bad person.

But I understand the concern. For some, the very existence of a pos- sible entanglement with the far right is a reason to be suspicious of any challenge to liberal values. For those who hold this position, members of the far left and members of the far right can appear to have the same fundamental problems: neither group is categorically opposed to violence, both seek out confrontation, and both priori- tize social and political intervention over the immediate rights of the individual.

I do not hold this position politically. I do not believe that antifascist and far-right militant groups can be equated, and I can give you argu- ments as to why. I can say that there is a clear distinction to be made between those who engage in violence in the name of retaining power and those who engage in violence in the name of protecting those who are already exposed to forms of structural violence. I can tell you that even if these groups share formal characteristics, their aims are clearly different. I can remind you that content matters.

But none of those arguments account for the fact that I am drawn to uncompromising positions not only because of my political convictions, but also because of the emotional solidarity I feel with uncompromising figures and the attraction I feel toward illiberal forms, from the polarizing rhetoric of manifestos to the brutality of minimalist sculpture, from the strident aesthetic of punk to the categorical abstraction of the Russian avant-garde.

It is on this level, on the level of affect and aesthetics, that I am sympathetic to the feeling of unease one might have about the closeness of the left and the right when it comes to the critique of liberalism. I am sympathetic with that unease, because I have felt the pull of fascist aesthetics. I felt it most strongly as a child, when I first found freedom unsatisfying.

I was raised in a community in which many of our parents had been either social activists or members of the counterculture in the 1960s. Portland, Oregon, was a destination for people of this type as the '60s waned, a retreat from the high cost of living and congestion of Los Angeles and San Francisco, a place to settle down and have kids. I was one of these children, a second-generation countercultural colonizer of a working-class logging town.

My early childhood education institutionalized the ethos of '60s social critique. We were subject to experiments such as "Mathematics Their Way," in which we were supposed to play creatively with blocks instead of being taught how to add on paper. Experiments like "Daily Oral Language," in which the teacher would put a sentence, riddled with errors, on the overhead projector and ask us to call out—no raising hands necessary—things we would like to do to the sentence, things that we believed would make it better.

But we didn't know anything. So we played with blocks and placed commas willy-nilly in broken phrases and learned nothing. We guessed at grammar. Our unreadable handwriting was a beautiful reflection of our uniqueness. We assembled rafts with dried beans, glue, and Popsicle sticks, and were told to look at them and think about what the number one hundred *meant to us*.

I was frustrated; I wanted to learn something. But I was no match for my teachers, who demanded that I be free. *Go explore!* they implored. *Play! Be yourself!*

Miserably searching for some form of order, I found structure in voluntary worksheets and old reading textbooks with quizzes at the end of every chapter. Some of the most worn ones contained endless, repetitive problem sets. I worked through them unit by unit, from pretest to post-test, until free time was over and I had to go to recess.

Meanwhile, our educational films taught us about the danger of centralized power and violence. My very favorite was the 1981 Afterschool Special *The Wave*. *The Wave* dramatizes the true story of a history teacher who, in the late 1960s, started an authoritarian movement at his high school. During a unit on Nazi Germany, a student asks him how it was that Germans allowed the extermination of 10 million people to occur in their midst. The teacher decides to show them. He begins a program called The Wave in which he trains his students in strict discipline. He rewards them for sitting up straight, standing when they address him, and responding to his instructions without complaint.

He invents a symbol. A salute. A chant.

Strength through discipline. Strength through community. Strength through action, his students intone, pounding their chests.

Watching the film again now, on a tiny two-by-three-inch YouTube window, I feel chills running pleasantly through my body, just as they did thirty years ago.

There is one student who refuses to take part: Laurie, the good girl, the one who knows all the answers at the film's beginning, the one who doesn't need a movement to feel successful.

Laurie publishes articles critical of The Wave in the school newspaper. She is stalked. Nearly beaten by her ex-boyfriend. And she does the thing that all good girls do when they disapprove of the actions of their peers: she tells the teacher. The teacher, however, is busy playing the part of the dictator. His students are finally listening to him. Close-up shots of his face reveal his sadistic pleasure in a raised eyebrow; a slight, almost imperceptible, smile.

I was very much a Laurie when I first saw *The Wave*. The teacher's number one helper. The one who would report on her peers at the slightest sign of disobedience. And yet, I don't recall identifying with her.

The thrill of The Wave was too strong. I wanted those students to chant forever. To go further. There could be uniforms. Songs. Marches. The mob could get bigger, the chants louder.

You've got to stop this nightmare, Laurie pleads, right around the thirty-two-minute mark.

You're right. And I will. the teacher responds.

Wait! I want to yell out. *Why does it all have to end so quickly?*

The moral of *The Wave* was intended to be the same as the message behind my elementary education: Be an individual. And more: To be a Laurie, to be a good girl, is to be an individual. To speak out. To refuse to be subsumed by the collective.

But what I liked about *The Wave* was the opposite of all of that. The beautiful synchronized chants. The once slacker students standing at attention. And when I was a Laurie, what I wanted most was not to exercise my individuality; what I wanted was something more like The Wave movement itself. I wanted structure; organization; form.

<><><>

In a 1975 essay on fascist aesthetics, Susan Sontag observes that an attraction to fascist symbolism is a particular type of sadomasochistic fantasy, one that draws on social history rather than individual psychology. She wonders if the rise of fascist iconography in her moment could be seen as a mass sadomasochistic reaction, a collective erotic "response to an oppressive freedom of choice . . . to an unbearable degree of individuality."

She might be right. But the oppressive freedom of choice she identifies has a particular historical context. There are moments in the essay when Sontag appears to blame subcultures for this condition, locating particular susceptibility to the lure of fascist forms in queer subcultures and the burgeoning punk scene. This seems odd to me now, given that members of these groups often, for reasons of sexuality and class, had diminished access to real choices. But in the mid-1970s, Sontag likely had only a faint glimmer of how it was that subcultures could falsely appear to be at the wheel in this process; how the gains of the social movements of the 1960s were at that moment being marshaled to support the implementation of neoliberal economic policies;

how the call for freedom from oppression was being twisted to look like a call for free markets.

In his book *A Brief History of Neoliberalism*, the scholar David Harvey offers a convincing account of this process. Because, he writes, the 1960s social movements were so focused on freedom as a value, the institution of neoliberal policies in the 1970s and '80s—policies that included union busting, privatization of public resources, the destruction of the social safety net, and so on—could be "backed up by a practical strategy that emphasized the liberty of consumer choice." The freedom to buy replaced appeals for freedom of expression and assembly, freedom from persecution by the state. Perversely, neoliberalism looked like the counterculture achieved by other means.

Sontag writes that fascist aesthetics "are perhaps only a logical extension of an affluent society's tendency to turn every part of people's lives into a taste, a choice."

I would add that the choices provided by this "affluent society" were mostly false choices, commercial choices premised on the furthering of the structural violence of capitalism. If neoliberalism substituted market freedom for freedom from structural inequality, the erotic pull of fascist aesthetics may be the consequence of the hollowness of that substitution. Or, put another way, fascist aesthetics emerge because neoliberalism produces, for its most privileged subjects, empty choices, empty freedoms. And the intolerability of living with that meaninglessness seeps into the presumed winners of the neoliberal game, creating a quiet form of misery that one can easily see spinning over into the suicidal logic of fascism.

"All efforts to aestheticize politics culminate in one point," writes Walter Benjamin during the German buildup to World War II. *"That one point is war."*

For Benjamin, aestheticizing politics means giving the masses opportunities for political expression without changing their fundamental structural conditions. You get marches and rallies, but not economic equality. You can have movies, posters, books, and newsletters, but not health care.

This is what fascism is, he argues: a political system that enables the masses to express themselves—their anger, their pride, their desire for change—without granting them any substantive rights. Fascism, for Benjamin, is therefore defined first and foremost as a form of aesthetic gratification, one that uses aesthetic pleasure to mask political questions about the distribution of power, of wealth, and of property.

War is the necessary outcome of this logic, as war takes industrial technology and uses it to produce a violent spectacle rather than social change. To illustrate this point, Benjamin quotes the avant-garde poet F. T. Marinetti, whose manifesto on the war in Ethiopia reads:

> War is beautiful because it enriches a flowering meadow with the fiery orchids of machine-guns. War is beautiful because it combines gunfire, barrages, cease-fires, scents, and the fragrance of putrefaction into a symphony.

Humankind, writes Benjamin, has gotten to the point where it "can experience its own annihilation as a supreme aesthetic pleasure. *Such is the aestheticizing of politics, as practiced by fascism.*"

In my opinion, Benjamin's remains the best theory of fascism's appeal. Fascism creates the emotions, sensations, expressions, and aesthetics of revolt without challenging existing structural hierarchies.

McInnes, with his punk rock hipster variant of neofascism, is a useful illustration of this. Several articles have tried to make sense of his transition from his days as cofounder and publisher of *VICE* magazine, the periodical that served as a veritable hipster manual in the early

2000s, to his current status as an icon of the far right. Many of these pieces ask a question not unlike the one my friend asked me about McInnes: How is it that punk could be made to serve far-right values?

I think this is the wrong question to ask about McInnes. That's not to say that punk doesn't have right-wing, even Nazi, variants. I grew up with Nazi skinheads occupying some of the coveted all-ages nights at my favorite venue in town. Their bands sounded a lot like our bands; they even looked like our bands: mostly white men in boots and scrappy T-shirts, hair buzzed short. But they couldn't be confused with one another. Our bands didn't openly espouse racial genocide. Theirs did.

But McInnes's version of punk wasn't that one: McInnes was part of the general emptying of punk of any kind of ideological content, leaving only style without even a vague, even a nominal, subcultural referent.

I hated VICE magazine in its early days because it epitomized the fuck-it party ethos of the turn of the millennium in New York. This was the height of '80s nostalgia and American Apparel; of trucker hats and ironic T-shirts; of the Strokes and go-go boots. The hipster as type arrived in this moment in its full expression: as someone who could display opposition to the mainstream in style, manner, and fashion, but who, at the same time, could openly profess no interest in challenging any concrete aspect of the status quo. This was punk stripped even of its most fundamental, abstract, unchained ethos of refusal. The hipster signaled the total detachment of punk style from politics.

Or, as Douglas Haddow, writing at the height of hipsterism, in 2008, puts it: "While previous youth movements have challenged the dysfunction and decadence of their elders," hipsters are "a youth subculture that mirrors the doomed shallowness of mainstream society."

Hipsterism isn't a compromise; it's not an uneasy reconciliation between a counterculture and the market. It's a total, thoroughgoing celebration of capitalism wrapped in the sheerest tissue of rebelliousness.

It's not a coincidence that the hipsters of the '00s embraced nostalgia for the 1980s above all other decades. If you went into any bar on the Lower East Side or in Williamsburg in 2004, you could easily imagine you were on the set of a John Hughes film, surrounded by tight-jeans-wearing, cigarette-smoking, Lycra-clad, mulletted, baseball-hatted, cropped-shirt-wearing, big-haired, upper-middle-class white adolescents. The only difference would be the added confidence that only self-ironizing can offer.

And *VICE* was the magazine that epitomized that moment. For those looking for explicit political consistency in McInnes's biography, it can be found in the magazine's early articles, which were often misogynistic, homophobic, and racist. But rather than being put forward as political arguments, these positions were taken in the name of sarcasm, of smashing pieties, of refusing to play by the rules. Using offensive slurs and representing exaggerated racial, sexual, and gendered stereotypes were, within the system of hipsterism, ways of establishing one's difference from the mainstream. One wasn't to take them seriously; to do so was to be a grown-up, a member of the establishment. For Haddow, this means that "the hipster represents the end of Western civilization—a culture lost in the superficiality of its past and unable to create any new meaning. Not only is it unsustainable, it is suicidal."

The hipster arrived at a moment in which people in the United States and Europe with access to a certain level of privilege did begin to experience *an unbearable degree of individuality.* Hence the low stakes of hipster identification: one would never be socially excluded for wearing an ironic trucker hat or a low-cut neon unitard, because all styles, even the most ridiculous, even the most historically edgy, had become permissible. But this permission resided only in the aesthetic sphere.

Hipsterism gave the masses aesthetic forms of expression without structural change: Benjamin's definition of the aestheticization of politics.

Fascism, of the kind we see gestured toward in groups like McInnes's Proud Boys, merely required that the underlying rationale of the hipster be pushed toward its logical conclusion. If aesthetics becomes the terrain of all rebellious imagining and if politics no longer matter, it makes sense that some people would be inclined toward charismatic leaders such as McInnes and other far-right YouTube celebrities; empty in-group rituals, such as the Proud Boys' initiation, which consists of reciting the names of five breakfast cereals while being punched repeatedly in the face; and a turn to violence, such as the Charlottesville marches and murder.

"Can the hipster, by virtue of proximity if nothing else, be woken up?" Mark Greif asks this question in his 2010 essay "What Was the Hipster?" He is imagining a countercultural formation that will follow hipsterism, one that might have meaningful political attachments. And in some cases, this happened. By the 2010s, some of the PBR-chugging Williamsburg set would participate in Occupy, Black Lives Matter, and feminist actions associated with #MeToo.

But, in other cases, the hipster woke up in a political direction that Greif never imagined.

It shouldn't have been surprising that after a decade of bored kids in trucker hats, we would see some of those kids become attracted to a much more intense form of expression: a night march with torches. And that's why, what with McInnes's postpunk style, Richard Spencer's long-on-top, shaved-sides haircut, and Milo Yiannopoulos's glam party-boy look, it can be hard to tell the difference between a hipster and a white supremacist, which can make it appear as if subcultural forms of refusal no longer hold any meaning.

But the notion that there is no longer a meaningful form of refusal is the suicidal cause, not the consequence, of this strange convergence. Because throughout all of this, one thing remains consistent:

the empty individualism that neoliberalism produces in its most privileged subjects.

<><><>

The Wave gave me a thrill, but its attraction quickly faded.

Why? Because even if I wouldn't have put it this way, I could tell the difference between art that was committed to changing what was intolerable and art that merely made my intolerable present more exciting.

Fascist aesthetics are one response to *an unbearable degree of individuality,* or at least individuality of a certain kind: the kind produced by capitalism. But they aren't the only response. Even if art is not the same as politics, not all works of art aestheticize politics in a way that obscures the possibility of structural change. I think of Paul Beatty's satire and the way it makes covert forms of racism visible. I think about Rankine's experiment with abstraction as a critique of the police. I think about Lerner's self-interrogation, which criticizes contemporary capitalism for the damage it causes to art.

None of these works of art by themselves change the world, but they do manage to be more than mere ornaments for the structural violence that underlies neoliberal capitalism. And they aim a critique at one of the most fundamental belief structures that supports our current system: the liberal notion that the primary social function is to elevate the individual over the collective.

11

MY NEIGHBOR'S HEART

It's November 2016, and I'm not in the streets. I'm not in the class-room. I'm on sabbatical, which means I'm being paid a salary that exceeds the median wage of my neighbors' to sit in my house and read and write about books.

Most days I feel ridiculous, like some parody of a self-important aca-demic, like George Eliot's Edward Casaubon and his interminable work on his would-be scholarly masterpiece, *Key to All Mythologies*. Or Jennifer Egan's satire of the depressed professor Uncle Ted, whose idea of work is locking himself in his office to "sit and think about art."

All of the season's prizewinning novels are sitting in a pile on my desk. I have no interest in reading them. Strangely and suddenly indifferent to literature of any kind, I feel like Ben Lerner's protagonist Adam, in *Leaving the Atocha Station*, who is obsessed with watching other people in museums who seem to be having a "profound experience of art," be-cause he is baffled as to how such a thing is possible.

I hunger for some kind of immediacy, some kind of real-world rele-vance, but I can make sense of my situation only through literary ref-erences. Trained in narrative analysis, I am devastatingly aware of this particular example of situational irony.

While I sit in my house in St. Louis with my sad stack of books, my neighbor hangs out on the front porch across the street with a group of white men in crisp polo shirts and baseball hats. They drink beer in koozies with American flags on them. *A cabal*, I mumble to my spouse.

He nods, and adds, *and given what we know about the gun laws in this state,*
it's probably an armed cabal.

I imagine that they are making preparations. Readying themselves to
defend their friends. And me? How am I preparing?

There are champions of the arts and the humanities who would have
an answer. They would say I am preparing by reading and writing
about art. That engaging with beauty, with thought, with the best that
humans have produced, is an important form of cultivation, but one
that is the opposite of what I fear in my neighbor and his cabal. They,
I worry, are preparing for war. I, these cultural optimists might argue,
am training myself in the art of peace. For seeing the potential in humanity. For developing empathy for individuals that transcends categorical distinctions.

I feel about this argument the way Stephen Dedalus feels about religion in James Joyce's *A Portrait of the Artist as a Young Man.* I cannot
muster the faith I need to support it, but I am terrified of what is in
store for me without it.

I know that my fear of my neighbor and his friends is irrational. And yet
I cannot shake the sense that my friends, my environment, my work—
everything I love—are under assault.

In the impulse buy section of my local bookstore, I find Brooke
Gladstone's book *The Trouble with Reality.* It promises to explain my
wretched feelings, to tell me why I have become suspicious, bitter, and
paralyzed with dread. Jad Abumrad, host of one of my favorite podcasts, has a blurb on the back. It says: "I read this in one sitting, and
at the end, for a fleeting moment, felt like I had a new hammer in
my hand."

I need that hammer. I buy the book. Once I'm back in my office, I open it to the first page:

"Perhaps you picked up this book because an icy hand grips your viscera; sometimes squeezing, sometimes easing, always present."

Yes, I think. *YES.*

I read the book hungrily, the way I used to consume novels, the way I haven't read for months. I learn about the concept of *umwelt*, a notion that originates from biologist Jakob von Uexküll. As Gladstone summarizes it, Uexküll was interested in how to describe the fact that "different animals living on the same patch of earth experience utterly disparate realities." A bird and a squirrel might share a tree, but the bird's tree and the squirrel's tree are, in essence, separate realities because their perceptions, orientations, needs, and sensory capacities are so different. Those separate realities are their *umwelts*.

Drawing from neuroscientific studies of the strength of political feelings, Gladstone argues that political partisanship has developed into a division of our species into two distinct *umwelts*. This suggests that those on the left and those on the right now live in entirely different realities. And any disturbance to those realities—say, the revelation that a significant number of my neighbors are entirely and unshakably devoted to a leader who espouses blatantly racist, xenophobic, sexist views—is so destabilizing on the level of the physiological operation of the organism that the brain will go through any number of complicated narrative operations to protect the organism from the intervention of counterrealities. If these narrative operations fail, the organism is left with panic. *An icy hand grips the viscera.*

Knowing this about partisan *umwelts* means we can better understand why many of us feel so alienated from others. It means that my neighbor and I process our daily experiences so differently that we could be considered to live in separate but overlapping worlds, the way a tick and a bloodhound might share a space but process that space so differently as to essentially have no common sensory experiences.

I suddenly realize something disturbing. Not about my neighbor, but about me.

I realize that I think of my neighbor as belonging to a different species.

I feel this way when I see him strutting down the sidewalk, beer belly pressed against his T-shirt, mustache hanging over his upper lip like a stunned gerbil, shouting at his grandkids and gesturing broadly as if he owned the street, suggesting with everything about him, his posture, his voice, his mean stare, that anyone who is not white, male, Christian, and heterosexual is an idiot or a threat, and I think—I'm sorry, I can't help it—*I have more in common with my dog than I do with this man. I welcome the extinction of his species. It cannot come soon enough.*

I think this even though I recognize this precise thought as the kind of thought that has given justification for genocides and therefore could be seen as a direct cause of the murder of twelve members of my family on my mother's side at Auschwitz and elsewhere.

I am as disturbed by my own genocidal fantasies as I am by my neighbor and his cabal. My entire *umwelt*, it seems, is falling apart. I need that hammer that Jad Abumrad found in his hand. I read on, looking for a solution.

Gladstone concludes by arguing that once we know the degree to which our realities diverge, it is "our obligation as citizens . . . to repair and improve the nation in which we live."

I throw the book down in despair. Isn't the whole point of *umwelt* the recognition that one partisan group's reality might be virtually impenetrable by attempts to call it into question? That facts and reason can go only so far in addressing firmly held beliefs about how the world works?

Gladstone, it seems, has written herself into a dead end. But despite my frustration, I cannot help but empathize with her inability to think outside of the *umwelt* constructed by her own liberal humanist training.

It is at this precise crisis point, where reasoned argument fails, that art is supposed to sweep in and save the day. Literature has long been imagined to be able to alter its readers by compelling empathy, by putting readers in touch with universal human feelings. These feelings, the argument goes, bring readers back to the foundational truth of what it means to be a human being. Divisions among us should melt away in the face of literature's affective reminder of our commonality. We should become more sensitive, more generous, more able to enter the worlds of others. The boundaries of our *umwelts* should become visible to us, and therefore more permeable.

The philosopher Martha Nussbaum observes that "very often in today's political life we lack the capacity to see one another as fully human." The source of our problems, she argues, is a view of the world that imagines people as fulfilling structural roles rather than having unique individual identities. This view dehumanizes others, which is dangerous and antidemocratic.

But she says that there is a solution: literature, with its access to certain humanizing emotions, can remind us that each human is not reducible to a type. Literary emotions enable us to see past our categorical assumptions. They rehumanize us and therefore reenergize democracy, which relies upon the acknowledgment of legitimate difference.

"Because it summons powerful emotions," she writes, "[literature] disconcerts and puzzles. It inspires distrust of conventional pieties and exacts a frequently painful confrontation with one's own thoughts and intentions." Reading literature, according to Nussbaum, alters us. And that alteration can make us better citizens.

Nussbaum's argument stands in a long tradition. Because liberalism values the individual above everything else, it requires an account of how individuals can be encouraged to care for one another. The arts have often played that imagined role. For Lionel Trilling, "literature is the human activity that takes the fullest and most precise account of variousness, possibility, complexity, and difficulty," values that are fundamental to liberalism's affirmation of individual freedom insofar as they work against the tendency for liberalism's laws and procedures to turn into rigid bureaucratic control.

According to this tradition, the fact that I spend many hours of my days reading literature should make me more open, more optimistic, more suspicious of limits to my thinking, and willing to entertain perspectives that differ from my own. Exposure to literature should have shaped me in a way that would challenge the rigidity of my *umwelt*.

I imagine that a friend of mine, also a literature professor, is feeling something along these lines when, after listening to me rant about my neighbor's offensive behavior, she suggests that I show up on his doorstep with cookies. *It's the holidays, you know. Maybe you could find some common ground.*

I'm not in the habit of baking white supremacists cookies, I snap, unaware of the hostility in my voice until I see my usually unflappable friend wince.

I am disappointed in myself. And even more, I am disappointed in literature. It has not done for me what it was supposed to do. I am not a better person for all the hours I have spent reading.

Is it possible, I wonder, *that literature could have made me worse?*

Gladstone's book is compelling to me because she describes contemporary political partisanship as I experience it: not as a rational disagreement, but as an embodied sensation that runs against all reason, one that I experience as unpleasant because it feels out of my control. I know that this sensation takes me further away from the parts of myself that are generous and forgiving, the parts of myself that are good.

There is a line of thinking, however, that would say that I have this all backward. That it is my very desire to be good, not my inability to be civil, that makes my rage so potentially destructive.

Friedrich Nietzsche, for instance, argues that *ressentiment*—his term for bad conscience or guilt—is the prevailing attitude of modern Western societies. And, for him, that attitude is the consequence of the myth of the liberal social contract. Liberal societies, which no longer rely upon strict hierarchies and the threat of force, require the suppression of instincts and the privileging of moral values such as restraint, modesty, and prudence. These are feelings Nietzsche associates with "the morbid softening and moralization through which the animal 'man' finally learns to be ashamed of all his instincts." The consequences for this, he argues, are dire: the rise of morality, shame, and *ressentiment* leads to a turning of humanity's animal violence inward, and this constitutes a nihilistic, almost suicidal, turn away from life. He believes this turning inward of violence leads to hatred and bitterness: dangerous feelings that stem from the doomed attempt to be good.

This resonates with my experience, with the danger I see in the substitution of morality for a structural account of power. But when I get a taste of what Nietzsche has in mind as an alternative to liberalism, I don't like it. I especially don't like the oft-quoted passages in which he argues that a "blond beast" will rise and destroy the weak once and for all, or those in which he seems to suggest that some people are meant to be predators and others prey.

I feel similarly ambivalent about Nietzsche's reflections on art. Art's power, he suggests, is residual of presocial instincts; it is a bubbling up of all that is repressed in the modern social order. This is because art is allied with a certain kind of "boldness": "mad, absurd, and sudden in its expression." Those who possess this characteristic, allied with the spirit of the artist, can be recognized through "their indifference to and contempt for security, body, life, comfort, their hair-raising cheerfulness and profound joy in all destruction, in all the voluptuousness of victory and cruelty."

This definition of art anticipates a broader rhetoric of avant-gardism that will flourish in the early twentieth century that also runs against the liberal tradition. The avant-gardist impulse, according to Peter Bürger, is defined by the effort to merge art and life in such a way that art might forcefully change reality. The result of this effort, however, as Maggie Nelson observes in *The Art of Cruelty*, is the tendency for avant-gardists to embrace violence. "Precision, transgression, purgation, productive unease, abjectness, radical exposure, uncanniness, unnerving frankness, acknowledged sadism and masochism, a sense of clearing or clarity"— these are all strategies that, as Nelson notes, are hallmarks of avant-gardism. But, she argues, they can also easily turn over into cruelty.

The feelings associated with art, in this view, are not at all like the liberal feelings of empathy and tolerance imagined by Nussbaum and Trilling. They are excessive, impersonal, violent, and animalistic. They heighten conflict. They deform and destroy. These are not the kinds of feelings that are conducive to compromises.

They are more like the feelings that might lead me to consent to the extermination of my neighbor and his cabal.

Or for me to lunge at him, teeth bared, fingers reaching for the throat.

<><><>

My neighbor had a heart attack two months ago. He disappeared suddenly and without explanation. It was very quiet. The block felt bigger without him taking up so much room.

A woman who lives farther down the block approached me with the news. *He's in the hospital. It doesn't look good,* she said with an expression I couldn't quite read.

But now my neighbor has suddenly reappeared on the block, a bit thinner, a bit paler, maybe a bit more subdued, but still loud. Swaggering. *It's a miracle!* he shouts.

He barks his story at a woman who has just returned from an errand with her new baby. He stands on her front steps, hands in pockets, pelvis thrust forward. One of her hands is on her front door handle, the other is shaking with the weight of her child. Her eyes dart side to side. She smiles nervously. Nods vaguely. The baby roots impatiently at her neck.

I am told that my neighbor now has an automatic defibrillator implanted in his chest. It will respond with healing shocks if his heartbeat shows any signs of irregularity.

The defibrillator becomes, in my worst moments, a metaphor for my neighbor's political *umwelt*: the impermeability of its protective mechanisms and the immortality those mechanisms provide.

Does this mean he can never die? I ask my partner, and we chuckle nervously, avoiding each other's direct gaze.

But in my better moments, the notion of "healing shocks" brings to mind the work of Theodor Adorno, and his guarded hopes for the shock of aesthetic experience to create social change.

"Aesthetic comportment," writes Adorno at the end of *Aesthetic Theory*, "is to be defined as the capacity to shudder." The shudder, for Adorno, occurs when art draws upon feelings that are not predicated upon the notion of the individual, feelings that were likely with us prior to the invention of anything like modern society. The shudder reminds us of the artificiality of our sense of ourselves as discrete individuals because it comes from a feeling of "being touched by the other" in a supremely vulnerable way. The shudder is what we feel when we have rolled onto our backs and exposed our bellies to the beast with the large mouth and sharp teeth. And yet, because the shudder happens in art, apart from society, the person who shudders is not literally threatened with annihilation. Art produces a sensation that indicates a momentary and mediated opening to others, one that need not result in violence.

This makes me think about how art and *umwelt* are connected, as John Dewey suggests they are when he argues that the "germ" of aesthetic experience is visible in moments of "heightened vitality." Rather than "being shut up within one's own private feelings," he writes, these moments are characterized by "active and alert commerce with the world" in which there is "complete interpenetration of self and the world of objects and events." In other words, art is born out of moments in which one's *umwelt* is stretched to encompass worlds outside of oneself, when the very notion of one*self* is challenged by awareness of one's small place in the larger connections among human and nonhuman things.

And maybe that's why many of my friends are artists, writers, critics, scholars, or just voracious readers. Their *umwelts* have been stretched, and they crave that stretching, seeking it out wherever they can. But the idea that one's lifeworld can get bigger, that it can encompass more and more complexity, is not the same thing as empathy, because it isn't about registering the specificity of individual emotional experience. And it's not the same thing as compromise, because radicality and extremity can be just as much a part of this broadening. Making something bigger doesn't mean it will come to the center.

For this reason, the literature and art that I encounter will not necessarily make my *umwelt* overlap with my neighbor's. And that's fine. I don't want my *umwelt* to be like my neighbor's. I'm not envious of his lifeworld. Nor do I care if his *umwelt* becomes like mine, though I do wish he would be less belligerent, chauvinistic, and mean.

I do not need my *umwelt* to overlap with my neighbor's, because I do not believe in a universal community of humankind. I know enough about the definition of the human—how it has been racialized, gendered, linked to states of physical ability, wealth, and labor—to be aware of how it has been employed to exclude and dehumanize as much as it has helped people come together.

I believe in the existence of friends and enemies. I know that politics is a matter of inclusion and exclusion, and my neighbor's political positions are positions that I want to exclude.

Recognizing this will help me turn away from my most violent thoughts. Because those are based on wanting to destroy my enemy, which, I realize, is a distraction born out of a moral conviction that I am good and he is bad. It is a distraction because it takes me away from what might be the real political achievement of art, one that has nothing to do with morality.

By expanding our *umwelts*, by taking us outside of ourselves and into the world, art is political when it helps us commit to the urgency of protecting, caring for, and enabling our friends.

12

COMPROMISE IN LOCKDOWN

When the lockdown order comes in, my first thought is: *I am ready.* Its strictness suits me. For once, no compromise. My love of form, my distrust of half measures and the idiosyncrasy of individual choice, it all seems perversely vindicated. The pandemic is revolutionary, even if it is brutally so. It makes the impossible possible. It justifies extremity. It exposes the limits of capitalism, of liberal individualism, of freedom.

The lived reality is more complicated. The lockdown seems uncompromising because the social behavior it necessitates is so crushingly total. But every day there are new problems to solve. My partner and I are among the lucky ones: the college classes we teach have gone online, and that means we don't need to make the hardest compromises, ones that involve trading risk for work, physical safety for basic needs. But we are still hounded by compromises—banal, obstinate, and exhausting. Schools have moved to remote learning, which our first grader cannot do alone. So work is a compromise, because it takes us away from our child. Being with our child is a compromise because it takes us away from work, emails piling up from students who are suddenly full-time caregivers and financial providers, forced to make their own impossible compromises in order to finish their degrees. The child needs us. Our students need us. We are compromising constantly, having to come face-to-face with our inevitable failures, in order to uphold a larger principle, one that cannot be compromised on: the principle of saving as many lives as possible, even as the deaths have already begun to mount.

Lawn signs in my neighborhood say YOU GOT THIS! and DON'T GIVE UP! The signs are meant to be uplifting, but they make me feel as though I'm at the back of the pack in a 5k race and should be mustering my competitive spirit, showcasing my endurance. There is a sense of desperation and dread about those signs, which can't help but signify all of the damage that necessitates such cheerleading in the first place. They say DON'T GIVE UP!, but what they really mean is HERE COME THE SAD TIMES.

I am not ready for the sad times because I am a privileged child of the 1990s, the decade that was supposed to usher in an era of global freedom, prosperity, and peace. Despite everything I know, despite everything that has happened since, I cannot shake the part of my *umwelt* that tells me history happens elsewhere, that big social problems can be solved in a manner that keeps the comfort of my daily life intact, that maintains my economic, racial, and national privilege. "The endless solving of technical problems," said neocon Francis Fukuyama in 1989, describing what he believed life would be like after the end of history, the end of large-scale conflict. He thought that the end of the Cold War—"an unabashed victory of economic and political liberalism"— meant that the big political questions had been answered. All that was left, he believed, was to manage the status quo.

I have always despised Fukuyama's worldview and everything it erases—the spoils of colonialism, the exploitation of global capitalism, the enduring violence of war and policing, the existence of friends and enemies, the continued need for political struggle—but it is part of my fundamental constitution to assume that my comfort will endure. The lockdown is a sign that all problems can't be solved, and that terrifies me, even as I feel history beginning to crack open, and a new way of life beginning to seem possible.

And there is more: the lockdown is uncompromising only because the virus is uncompromising. I can't help but admire the virus for its stubbornness, its refusal to cooperate. It will not *just be reasonable*. It doesn't care that there are *gray areas*. It will not *live and let live*. It does not believe that there is *a solution that will work for everyone*. Yet while the virus is not interested in individual choice, it is also not interested in justice. And because we live in an unjust society, the virus follows the logic of that society, exaggerating existing disparities based on wealth and race.

Part of me welcomes the lockdown, because I want a different world, and for the first time in my life a different world looks as if it might be imminent. But as I scroll through images of cars lined up at food banks and coffins lined up at crematoriums, I'm not at all sure that I want to live through what it might take to get there.

<><><>

During these early weeks, the actress Ellen DeGeneres says that being under a lockdown order is like being in jail, and she receives the appropriate backlash.

The experience of lockdown, as an economically secure person living in the United States, is not like being in jail, because when you are in jail you cannot wake up, have a cup of coffee on your back deck, and watch the magnolia blossoms wave exuberantly in the wind.

You cannot crawl into your child's bed in the morning, as I do, and hold her warm body close to yours, telling yourself that you are calming her when in reality you are calming yourself, her puffy little fingers sweeping along your cheeks.

You cannot walk your dog in the park, charting wide half-moon paths into the grass to maintain distance from others, the colors of spring emerging in shifting palates every day, green coming up in slow motion from grass to shrubs to small trees and finally into the branches of the two-hundred-year-old sycamores that shade the park's perimeter.

You cannot receive a bag of produce on your porch from a man in a fabric mask whose eyes you think you recognize from another world; one in which you stabbed slices of tomato with a toothpick out of a shared bowl at the farmers market, pressed shoulder to shoulder with strangers, thumb flesh glancing against tomato flesh, your microbiome one of hundreds rubbing against that vibrant red skin.

"There's a difference between what people like Ellen DeGeneres mean when they say *jail* and when they say *prison*," a friend says, weighing in on DeGeneres's comment. She doesn't mean the legal difference, jail as confinement before conviction, prison as confinement after. She means that *jail* is a term that has become detached from the material conditions of the criminal justice system. "When privileged people say *jail*," she continues, "it just means *not getting what you want. Prison* is something else: it's where people are dying of the virus."

My friend's explanation helps me understand how my rejection of compromise—compromise as a value, as a way of appealing to moderation, as a way of rejecting radical answers—relates to actual on-the-ground compromises. What DeGeneres is feeling when she says *jail—not getting what you want*—is what actual compromise feels like; it's what happens when you have to give something up for a greater good, for a larger principle, for something more important than yourself. But when compromise is understood as an end rather than a means, it promises to be more than that: compromise is supposed to solve problems and maintain stability such that no one needs to feel substantial loss. Of course what this means in practice is the maintenance of hierarchies, the preservation of power. Because people do lose in all compromises; it's just a matter of who feels it.

In order for people in positions of privilege to experience *not getting what [they] want* persistently, broadly, and socially, something has to be amiss that goes beyond the ideology of compromise. Something that takes society as a whole beyond the notion of moderation, beyond the technocratic solving of problems. There has to be some context forcing that condition that is absolutely uncompromising. Something like a virus. Or a lockdown order. Or an economic collapse. Or a revolution.

The lockdown begins with this sudden exposure of privileged people to *not getting what [they] want*, which is to say, to an experience that *feels like jail* because it feels like intolerable deprivation, scarcity, and loss of freedom. And the lockdown orders will begin to be lifted a few months later, as the nation confronts a much more profound loss: the murder of George Floyd.

Please, he will say, the police officer's knee on his neck. *Please. I can't breathe.*

Floyd's words will echo the words of Eric Garner, murdered by a police officer's chokehold six years earlier. Then, too, the phrase *I can't breathe* held significance beyond the physiological. *I can't breathe* described the sensation of being strangled by a system based on the exploitation of racialized people: by the extraction of wealth from their bodies, by their imprisonment and policing, by their use as care workers and emotional laborers even as they are deprived of care and support by the very institutions they serve, by the maintenance of their economic subjugation through deliberate legal, economic, and cultural means.

When Floyd utters these words on camera, they will carry with them all of these valences, and add to them the horrors of the virus, how it literally deprives the lungs of oxygen, but also how non-white Americans are disproportionately infected and dying.

We will eventually learn that Floyd was infected with the virus. But this only literalizes what *I can't breathe* already expresses, the reality that underlies capitalism but is usually hidden: how the security of the economically privileged is guaranteed by the persistent exposure of the economically insecure to bodily risk.

The lockdown forces a recognition of universal human loss and personal hardship. And within two months, the largest mass uprising for civil rights in American history will take place. They are horrible things: this virus, this murder. But their convergence leads to a sudden outpouring of solidarity, as if, for the beneficiaries of racial capitalism, *not getting what you want* is some kind of necessary prelude to political action.

<><><>

Lockdown might be a stunning and wide-ranging social experiment, a capital-*H* Historical Event, but I spend it mostly in meetings, making the usual ugly compromises, trying to help manage the catastrophe of the university budget, the deficit climbing by millions every day.

I once asked my sister, a practiced community organizer, how to run a meeting. She told me to bring food. When I balked, she explained that people need to feel as if they are in a situation of abundance in order to come to consensus. And the presence of food is a biological trigger; it makes us all feel like there are plenty of resources to go around.

Alternatives to capitalism are often portrayed in a capitalist culture as situations of scarcity. There is a certain blue filter that television shows use when they want to shift from a scene located in a liberal capitalist society to a scene located in a communist one, especially the Soviet Union. The filter creates a feeling of permanent, fallow winter. It turns everyone's face a pallid gray. That blue filter signifies that characters will not get what they want.

The lockdown seems to set a blue filter over the United States. Consumer spending is slowed to a trickle; grocery items are subject to rationing; so much wage labor is prohibited. But there are moments during the lockdown in which I feel as if I can see the potential abundance waiting beyond capitalism. There are mainstream calls for a basic income, for free health care. Community organizations offer direct aid. Global supply chains are supplanted with local food networks. Farmers drop eggs on porches; neighbors put bundles of kale out in their front yards, price: a recommended donation. Furloughed HR managers sew thousands of masks for health-care workers. Anarchist groups chalk instructions on the sidewalk on how to give and get money. At 3:00 p.m. on a sunny Tuesday, the park has never been so full.

I look at all the people out in the breezy March afternoon. They are reading books on blankets, playing Frisbee with their children, walking hand in hand with their lovers. I think: *what abundance.* And then I imagine their bank accounts draining, their bodies sealed to ventilators, and I know that the sad times are still coming.

I used to think that the only way that our society could fundamentally change would be through a catastrophe great enough to shake us all loose of our attachments to fixing things around the edges. I always imagined this future with dark ambivalence, knowing it would entail horrible loss even as it opened up new possibilities. But I also never bought into the postapocalyptic gloom of Cormac McCarthy's *The Road*, where the end of capitalism meant the end of society, and the destruction of our current form of social organization could end only in cannibalism and death cults. This has always struck me as conservative rhetoric, meant to protect a system in which scarcity seems imminent only because so many of the resources are currently concentrated in the hands of the few. I hoped that at some future date, those coffers might be opened, and a world of abundance would be possible.

Now the pandemic seems to fulfill my prophecy, at least the part about economic collapse. Nearly every data point is a crisis. Unemployment charts show jagged little teeth for a hundred years and then a sudden climb that takes the graph out of all proportion. I watch an animated version a friend shares on social media, and when that final spike begins, I feel a horrible dizzying vertigo rising with it, out of the limits of the graph, up and up and up. Where will this spike take us? I want to imagine that we can ride it into the end of capitalism, into the possibility of abundance, but the human cost is already overwhelming.

In a Zoom meeting I have with PhD students, the topic is adjunct labor. Just a few months ago, our conversations were about the objectionable working conditions of adjunct instructors: the low pay, the precarious semester-to-semester contracts, the lack of institutional support or identity. Now the conversation is about the cutting of adjunct funds as a consequence of pandemic-fueled budget shortfalls, the likelihood that those who eked out a living by driving from campus to campus, teaching five, six, seven classes per semester at three different institutions, will lose all opportunities for work. The abolition of adjuncts once seemed like a utopian dream; now it is a devastating reality. I squint at the grid of faces, trying to see who is crying. Most are on mute. Some are just black squares. Some look stoically at me, or at the camera, or perhaps at themselves. I say absurd things like *we will all do our best to protect the adjunct budget.* I say this because while I want this system to crumble, I cannot bear the sight of the suffering who are buried in the rubble.

I feel trapped between ethics and politics. Ethically, I believe that it is right to make every technocratic compromise available to restore stability and save the lives that are spiraling into emotional and physical danger. Politically, I think this is a rare opportunity to act only on larger principles, to allow the system to collapse, and to build something better, a system not based on exploitation, resource hoarding, and competition.

I cannot celebrate this crisis, because people are dying. They are dying of the virus, but they are also dying from inequality: from lack of health care, from deaths of despair, from uneven exposure to risk. But I also cannot nostalgically dream of the system's restoration, because to do so is to pretend that the price of the old way was not also paid quietly, month to month, in human suffering, pain, and death.

Inside the house, our lives revolve around the imperative to make the kind of compromises that maintain the status quo even as those compromises are becoming more and more impossible, more and more desperate. Every interaction holds the promise of a good day or a bad day. I think of happiness curves and pandemic curves and wonder, fleetingly, what the R0, or reproductive number, is of our happiness today and what tactics I can employ to move it above 1.0 so that its curve might sweep upward. And then there is the schedule, the monstrous thing I have built, its increasingly baroque grids, its formal insistence on back-and-forth, yours-and-mine, time parsed equally into little shares of work and care. It is all driven at maximizing the household happiness, of maintaining the mood curve, of avoiding the devastation of a sudden dive.

Maintaining the mood curve is difficult, because we are in a situation of scarcity. Of *you said you would be done by 2:00 so I could work and now it's 2:07.* Of *mama I'm lonely* and *I'm sorry not now sweetie I have to work.* Of *it's been a month and I haven't even looked at my book manuscript.* Of *professor can we please meet over Zoom tomorrow I have to talk with you my mother is sick.* Of empty shelves in the grocery store. Of sleepless nights tallying missed deadlines. Of our child curled up over her iPad, humming quietly to herself, three empty snack bowls surrounding her frame. Of my partner's grief over five years of work on a book that he fears will be released into a void. Of my grief over missing my parents, their voices strained on the phone as they promise again not to leave the house.

I imagine that I can bundle all of this loss and lift it over my head like Atlas. And then I imagine that the right compromises will allow me to squeeze it into a marble, place it in my palm, and show it to my family, saying, *see, it's nothing. It's so tiny.*

Because in comparison, it is. My spouse and I have spent our lives protected by the US security state, by our white privilege, by the financial cushion provided to us by our upwardly mobile parents. And now, in the midst of a global catastrophe, we are being only lightly brushed with what scarcity feels like. But, as an unbalanced monolith can be toppled by the lightest tap of a finger, this glancing touch of loss feels as if it could destroy us.

Two things are true: These feelings are genuine. But they also reveal a profound weakness cultivated by an unjust and unequal system. Those who are randomly assigned a place at the top of the hierarchy are lucky, but feeble, unpracticed as we are at survival, at grief, at the heartbreak of intractable problems that cannot be resolved through compromise.

<><><>

The lockdown order means no compromise. Compromising is coded as cheating. Either you obey or you cheat.

We are cheating, a friend confesses in a text. Their child is being cared for by someone not in their household so she and her partner can both work. I am struck by her use of the word, by its heavy moral weight.

Public health experts know that people will cheat. That is why they choose a modified lockdown over a military-enforced quarantine, because as anyone who knows anything about zombie plots is aware, if you put up a wall, someone will figure out how to break through.

During its early battle with the virus, China had strict quarantines, entire regions cut off from the rest of the country, and no-exception lockdowns enforced by police. Their leadership boasted in the press about the efficacy of authoritarianism, as liberal capitalist societies flailed against the complexity of civil liberties and governmental transparency. The US version of the lockdown order is a liberal solution to a pandemic, because it relies not on the rigidity of armed enforcement, which public health experts know will be resisted, but on the strength of fear and shame. It makes the liberal transformation that Schmitt wrote about back in the 1930s, turning the line drawing of politics into the individualism of morality.

My father tells me about his favorite mask-wearing public service advertisement, one in which a man stands maskless wearing a T-shirt that says THAT GUY. Everyone around him wears a mask and gives him the side-eye. DON'T BE THAT GUY, the ad proclaims. My father likes it because he thinks it is funny, but I can also hear it resonating more deeply with him, because despite the fact that he is a straight white man born in 1945 and therefore in the demographic most prone to being THAT GUY, he has always despised THAT GUY, and he takes pleasure, in everything from #MeToo to health PSAs, in seeing THAT GUY finally get his comeuppance.

The problem with the ad, however, is that it is morally tautological. If you care about not being THAT GUY, you probably don't need the ad at all. You're probably already wearing a mask. And in a pandemic, all it takes is one person who doesn't care if he's THAT GUY, or who takes pleasure in being THAT GUY, to begin an outbreak. And that is why a pandemic requires more than a moral plea for good people to behave correctly; it requires politics: a grappling with the complexities of power, self-governance, and law.

And yet, I think at first that this time moralization might actually work because the stakes are death, and the desire to not be a bad person is paired with a deep and chilling fear. But fear is fleeting. And shame, like all efforts to control social behavior with morality, can quickly turn over into self-righteous indignation and the celebration of transgression. So it makes sense when armed people show up at capitol buildings, governors' mansions, and statehouses across the country to demand the end of the lockdown, their masklessness a new partisan statement, like a bumper sticker or a message T-shirt, only lethal.

The face of the protest against lockdown measures is the far right, the rural white woman screaming for a hair appointment, her silver roots spelling out six weeks of shelter-in-place against the long mass of blond curls.

But the mainstreaming of the antilockdown argument comes quietly from many corners. *How long can we allow this to go on?* the argument is whispered over Zoom, over the phone, across fences, from sidewalk to front porch. *This is just not reasonable,* we all moan at some point or another. *Haven't we done enough?*

I say these things myself. Raised at the height of the technocratic imaginary, I, too, believe that there has to be a win-win solution, probably one that involves science (why is science so slow?) or entrepreneurial hustle (isn't there money to be made?).

Viruses are terrible negotiating partners, but we persist in bargaining. *I'll give you restaurants if you give me dentist appointments. I'll give you conferences if you give me elementary school.* But the virus refuses to compromise. It just infects, replicates, and kills.

After a few months, there appears to be a broad consensus among the voices amplified by major media outlets. The voices say *we've held up our part of the deal. We have washed hands and sewn masks. We have spent hundreds of hours on Zoom. We have changed our clothes at the door after work and showered in scalding water. We have argued with our children about inscrutable math problems and lost. We have watched, helpless, as they sleep until the afternoon, as their worlds narrow to a tiny screen. As our worlds narrow to a tiny screen. We have put on a happy face for grandparents and parents and aunts and uncles and brothers and sisters whom we haven't seen in months, might not see for years, might never see again.*

And that is why, though it is inconceivable during the early weeks of the lockdown, many people will begin to venture out only a few months later, against the recommendations of public health professionals. This will happen because so many of us have been trained that this is how compromises work: we have done our part, and on some level we believe, against all sanity, that the virus will do the same.

Of course the virus won't reciprocate. And maybe seeing this happen, being faced with an opposing party who really will not compromise, allows white people to get a glimmer of what racial injustice means. The experience of being repeatedly exposed to the threat of death no matter what you do may be novel to some, but for Black Americans it is a fundamental fact of existence. One can avoid walking outside at night. One can keep one's pockets empty, one's hands visible. One can be taught at an early age to say "yes, officer" and make no quick movements. But the police state can always respond with a bullet or a chokehold. Because when it comes down to it, deeply entrenched power hierarchies backed by force are a lot like viruses. There is no need for them to compromise, because they have the power to kill.

<><><>

The grocery store is terrifying and Instacart is on strike, so I try to give up perishables, stuffing my face with sliced bread and peanut butter, sliced bread and peanut butter, until moving my body in space feels like trying to lift my teeth out of a slice of bread covered in peanut butter: thick and grasping.

It might be all of the peanut butter or it might be the effort of managing the schedules. It might be the effort to be amenable, to *not give up*, to make things work. Whatever it is, my spouse and I are fighting more than usual, compromises failing, the family peace increasingly tenuous.

And then one day, a pandemic miracle: the farmers market begins weekly deliveries. I slot the moment the website goes live into the weekly schedule so I can refresh the page again and again and pounce on one of the precious two hundred produce boxes, scarcer than concert tickets.

The day the box comes is gray. We spend it driving from trailhead to trailhead trying to find somewhere to hike that is open and not crowded. The trail we find is muddy, and hikers pass too close. I jump off the trail, into the tick-covered brambles. He does, too, but more slowly. Sometimes he stands his ground, whether out of principle or distraction, I can't tell. Is it because space has begun to feel like a scarce resource? I grumble something passive-aggressive about gender, feeling the fire of moral self-righteousness rising. He snaps back, insisting that he *did move*, angry at the other hikers, furious at my criticism.

I stop looking at his face. On the drive home, I stare at my phone. Make plans for the following week. Answer work emails with the stock diplomatic phrases: *I am looking into this. Thank you for letting me know. We will try to accommodate your request. I will get back to you. Thanks for thinking of it.*

When we get home, the produce box is on the porch. I think: *At last. Abundance.* I bring it inside and as he is hauling backpacks and muddy boots I begin to hold up item after item, naming them proudly, my frenzy increasing with his marked silence: *Ozark mushrooms! Heirloom tomatoes!! Sunflower microgreens!!!* I wave the microgreens in his face, which has not changed. I try again: *SUNFLOWER MICROGREENS,* I yell, the bag of tiny tendrils swaying wildly in my right hand.

Nothing.

I slam the box down on the floor. I yell something like *I AM WORKING SO HARD TO MAKE US HAPPY* and he yells back that it isn't my job to make us happy as he hauls one of the seemingly endlessly proliferating piles of laundry upstairs.

Our child, compromiser in training, smiles brightly and says, *I want to see the sunflower microgreens, Mama!* I can't stand to look her in the eyes because I don't want to know how hard she is trying. Discouraged, she grabs a stack of books from the I Survived series (*I Survived the Sinking of the Titanic, 1912; I Survived the Great Molasses Flood, 1919; I Survived the Attacks of September 11, 2001*) and retreats to her room.

I start scrubbing the produce, imagining tenacious viral particles clinging to crevices in mushrooms, asparagus, radish greens. My shoulders are tight. I cannot remember when they didn't feel this way. It occurs to me: the effort I am putting into fixing something that cannot be fixed. *You got this,* the tension in my shoulders seems to say. But what I want to say back is: *maybe I don't.*

I go upstairs. I enter the room where he is angrily folding our child's PJs.

I sit on the floor. Dust bunnies swirl around me, coming to rest in gray tufts on my bare toes.

There are no compromises to strike, because compromise requires the belief that unsatisfactory things can be made satisfactory, at least temporarily. That the pain and loss generated by a bad situation can be managed, or made fair, or tolerable, even if the underlying conflict remains.

We have been trying to give things up to make each other happy, but in doing so we have made the mistake of so many compromisers: we have pushed away the reality of those unsatisfactory conditions, when we could have confronted them in all of their intractability, in all of their dread.

That confrontation is the core of what we call love. And it has nothing to do with compromise as a value, though the small compromises of everyday life, the give and take of living together, become so much easier in its wake.

For the first time in weeks, I reach out and touch his upper arm. I feel his cold skin taut against my fingertips. And then I feel it slowly warm to my touch and soften.

I try to soften, too, and when I do I wince at the harshness of what I am letting in: the loss of lives, of work, of friends, of family, all this loneliness, all this uncertainty. His embrace, too, when it comes, is heavy and sad. But it is also steadying. For the first time in months of being stuck together in the house, I don't feel alone.

<><><>

The lockdown orders expire one by one, which means nothing except that the state is retreating from responsibility. No more laws means no more checks. Free to work; free to starve; free to get sick; free to die.

And while working people feel the pull of the double bind that comes with the imposition of freedom, George Floyd is murdered in a shocking display of state violence, with millions of people watching.

The state will not impose an extended lockdown order because it will not provide resources to a population that cannot work. It will withhold those resources so that the population will say *we are in a situation of scarcity; we must work*. But the state will, as it turns out, use its resources with abandon when they are directed toward suppressing, beating, strangling, shooting, pepper spraying, and gassing a popular uprising against racism and capitalism. Suddenly, an abundance of tanks, shields, body armor, cuffs, Tasers, guns.

I hear my neighbor outside yelling about the protests *if you don't think you need an AR-15 right now, you're a fucking moron. These people are animals. They're coming for us.* He, too, is afraid of being in a situation of scarcity, despite his expensive leather boat shoes, his multiple properties, his enormous American flag.

At the march, we shout all of the phrases we have shouted for years, but as all strict forms do, they take on new meaning in a new context. We chant *shut it down* as we walk up the ramp, locking down Forest Park Parkway. We mimic the action of the state, but we do it for different reasons. Not to put the economy into what economist Paul Krugman described as a "medically induced coma," but to question the economy's origins and demand the redistribution of its spoils. Not to protect the bodies of the privileged, but to mourn the bodies that have been destroyed by racism, both overt and systemic.

And when we walk in the middle of the highway lanes, two thousand eyes made lazy with quarantine squinting in the sun, chanting *this is what democracy looks like*, what we mean is that democracy is made in conflict, in refusal, in actions that might seem excessive or extreme or too much, in the militant protection of those who are most vulnerable. We mean that democracy suffers when we are asked to compromise on our principles in advance in order to be practical, palatable, or un-threatening to those who want to maintain systems of injustice. We mean that democracy means confronting pain, looking suffering people in the face, and rejecting our impulse to think we can solve every prob-lem with a compromise.

Because sometimes we have to refuse to compromise, even though it is sad, even though it is scary. We have to change, to tolerate not getting what we want, to do so without the glamour and praise that come with moral sacrifice. We have to do it in the name of solidarity against racism and all forms of injustice, in the name of a democratic future in which compromises occur but are not held up as goals or values. Because in this future, the goal will be something uncompromising: the end of exploitation. And the end of exploitation will mean the end of scarcity, or at least its use to justify competition and violence.

I believe that we will win, the chant leader yells. And when I say it back, I try as hard as I can to mean it.

ACKNOWLEDGMENTS

This book is the outcome of conversations with friends, some of which are referenced directly in the text and others that provided me with insights that are not directly attributed.

I am grateful to those who read material from this book or helped me work through these ideas in conversation: Ellen Crowell, TJ DiFrancesco, Jesica Dolin, Bevin Early, Callie Garnett, Sean Grattan, Matt Hart, Mitchum Huehls, Devin Johnston, Emily Lordi, Sara Marcus, Melanie Micir, Daniel Poppick, Palmer Rampell, Helena Ribeiro, Jennifer Rust, Gabriel Solis, and Claire Wolford.

Daniel May introduced me to the work of Chantal Mouffe, which became central to my thinking about centrism and third-way politics. Joshua Kotin recommended Boris Groys's book on the Russian avant-garde. Andrew Marantz sent me links to disturbing alt-right videos and made me think harder about what I meant by illiberalism. I first learned about Margaret Anderson and the Reader Critic from a graduate school collaborative effort with Megan Ward.

Gloria Fisk brought the language of solidarity to this project and helped me understand what Ellen DeGeneres meant by "jail." Sarah Chihaya sent me text messages of obnoxious political message T-shirts until I had no choice but to write about selling out. She also helped me think more rigorously about Beyoncé's aesthetics of strength. Merve Emre ceaselessly reminded me that the core of this book was its insights about aesthetics. All three of these brilliant women, the best writing group anyone could wish for, read and gave feedback on multiple drafts of this project.

I am someone who is lucky to come from a family that supports me both emotionally and intellectually. My parents, Gary Smith and Marta Greenwald, and my sister, Sophie Smith, read this work, commented on it, and talked me through it, helping me navigate big questions from the practical to the existential.

Ted Mathys insisted that I could and should write this book. He caught examples of my arguments out in the world, especially in poetry, and brought them to me like little gifts. And he read countless drafts, coming to know my arguments in some ways better than I do.

Lucy Mathys-Smith appears here as thumb-wrestler, Phil Ochs–lover, and voracious reader of disaster narratives. She is all of these things. But she is also the person who has shown me that love means going toward suffering, rather than trying to fix it from a distance. "Compromise in Lockdown" is dedicated to her.

Many of the arguments in this book originated in essays that appeared in *The Account, Novel: A Forum on Fiction*, the *Los Angeles Review of Books, Post45 Contemporaries*, and *Post45: Peer Reviewed*. Many thanks to the editors and readers who helped me refine my thinking: Nancy Armstrong, Davis Smith-Brecheisen, Kinohi Nishikawa, Anna Shechtman, and Arthur Wang.

Parts of "Her Hand on My Octave" and "Bad People" appeared in a guest letter for a "Slow Burn" series in *Post45 Contemporaries* on Knausgaard's *My Struggle*. A brief part of "My Neighbor's Heart" appeared in "Tiny Books of the Resistance" in the *Los Angeles Review of Books*. I am grateful to Dan Sinykin and Lee Konstantinou for editing those pieces.

This project benefited from feedback received at several works-in-progress workshops and conferences. I am especially grateful to the organizers and participants at Post45 in Oxford, UK; Altered States at the Sorbonne in Paris; C21 at Washington University in St. Louis; the American Literature group at Harvard University; Reading in the Age of Trump in Mainz, Germany; and The Contemporary at Princeton University.

Adriana Duebel, Matthew Holder, Sydney Rice, Rachel Shields, and Collin Stansberry provided crucial research assistance. Toby Benis's leadership of the Saint Louis University English Department was indispensable to my ability to complete this project.

I am grateful to Graywolf Press for so many things—for taking a risk on this project, for welcoming me into a community of writers and thinkers, and for treating my work with respect and care. But paramount among all of these things is the rigorous editing I have received from Anni Liu, Yana Makuwa, Fiona McCrae, Susannah Sharpless, and Steve Woodward. I am also grateful to Katie Dublinski and the production team at Graywolf, as well as to Marisa Atkinson and the marketing team.

My work on this book was supported by a sabbatical, two Mellon Faculty Development Grants, and a Summer Humanities Research Award, all through Saint Louis University, as well as a Charles A. Ryskamp Research Fellowship through the American Council of Learned Societies.

WORKS CITED

Most of my textual references are quoted and attributed in the body of the text. When a text is attributed only to an author, the specific work can be found in this list. A few of my citations are drawn from multiple sources or require more explanation:

The quotations from *Poetry* magazine editor Christian Wiman appear in Dana Goodyear's article on the Lilly gift, "The Moneyed Muse," and the "warmed-over turkey" quote from Miles Davis appears in Ashley Kahn's piece "Miles Davis and Bill Evans: Miles and Bill in Black and White."

The analogy between formal constraint and break dancing in a strait-jacket that I reference in "In a Box" appears in several different inter-views with Terrance Hayes. The quotations I use are drawn from "Dinner with Terrance Hayes," an interview with Rachel Long published in the *White Review*, January 2019; and a recording of a Q&A after a reading at Politics and Prose Bookstore, in Washington, DC, on July 16, 2018.

The haiku in Claudia Rankine's *Citizen* has continued to evolve. The most recent edition reads, "Because white men can't / Police their imagi-nation / Black people are dying," substituting *men* in the third line with *people*. I have chosen to retain the previous version for its symmetry, even though I recognize the importance of clarifying the fact that many Black women, too, have been victims of police brutality and murder.

I first became aware of Karl Ove Knausgaard's interview with James Wood in the *Paris Review* from Omari Weekes's contribution to a "Slow Burn" series on Knausgaard. In a response to Weekes's piece, Diana

Hamilton wrote about the particular exchange I quote in "Bad People." You can read their work at *Post45 Contemporaries*, "The Slow Burn, v. 2: Summer of Knausgaard."

The archive in "A Riot of One" is the Riot Grrrl Collection at the Fales Library at New York University. The materials referred to in the chapter were drawn mostly from the Kathleen Hanna Papers, 1988–2005, and the Mark Anderson and Positive Force DC Riot Grrrl Collection, 1974–1998. Funding from the American Council of Learned Societies supported my time at the Fales.

<><><>

"A Letter on Justice and Open Debate." *Harper's Magazine*, 7 July 2020.
Adorno, Theodor. *Aesthetic Theory*. U of Minnesota P, 1970.
Ahmed, Sara. *The Cultural Politics of Emotion*. Routledge, 2004.
Anderson, Amanda. *Bleak Liberalism*. U of Chicago P, 2016.
Anderson, Margaret. "Announcement." *Little Review*, vol. 1, no. 1. March 1914.
———. "Our First Year." *Little Review*, vol. 1, no 11. February 1915.
———. "A Real Magazine." *Little Review*, vol. 3, no. 5. August 1916.
———. *My Thirty Years' War: An Autobiography*. Horizon P, 1982.
Artaud, Antonin. "The Theater and Cruelty." *The Theater and Its Double*. Grove P, 1958.
Ashton, Jennifer. "Totaling the Damage: Neoliberalism and Revolutionary Ambition in Recent American Poetry." Nonsite.org, 9 October 2015.
Baker, Elna. "It's a Small World After All." *This American Life*, Episode 589: "Tell Me I'm Fat." Podcast audio, 17 June 2016.
Baron, Zach. "Cary Fukunaga Doesn't Mind Taking Notes from Netflix's Algorithm." *GQ*, 27 August 2018.
Barr, John. "American Poetry in the New Century." Poetry Foundation, September 2006.
Battaglia, Andy. "Miles Davis *Kind of Blue: 50th Anniversary Edition*." *Pitchfork*, 6 October 2008.

Beatty, Paul. *The Sellout*. Picador, 2016.

Benjamin, Walter. "The Work of Art in the Age of Its Technological Reproducibility." *Selected Writings: Volume 4 1938–1940*. Translated by Harry Zohn and Edmund Jephcott. The Belknap P of Harvard UP, 2003.

Bennett, Eric. *Workshops of Empire: Stegner, Engle, and American Creative Writing during the Cold War*. U of Iowa P, 2015.

Boym, Svetlana. *The Future of Nostalgia*. Basic Books, 2002.

Bürger, Peter. *Theory of the Avant-Garde*. U of Minnesota P, 1984.

Burt, Stephanie (published under Stephen). "Close Calls with Nonsense." *Believer*, issue 13, 1 May 2004.

———. "A Response to Six Propositions on Compromise Aesthetics." *Account*, no. 1, Spring 2015.

Chen, Chris, and Tim Kreiner. "Free Speech, Minstrelsy, and the Avant-Garde." *Los Angeles Review of Books*, 10 December 2015.

Coates, Ta-Nehisi. "My President Was Black," *Atlantic*, January/February 2017.

Dewey, John. *Art as Experience*. Penguin Books, 1934.

Drucker, Johanna. *Sweet Dreams: Contemporary Art and Complicity*. U of Chicago P, 2005.

"Editors Talk Poetry Acceptances: Don Share, *Poetry*." *Frontier Poetry*, 6 March 2018.

Egan, Jennifer. *A Visit from the Goon Squad*. Anchor Books, 2011.

Eisenstein, Sergei. "A Dialectic Approach to Film Form." *Film Form: Essays in Film Theory*. Harcourt, Brace & World, 1949.

Everett, Percival. *Erasure*. Graywolf P, 2011.

Finnegan, William. "The Candidate." *New Yorker*, 31 May 2004.

Foucault, Michel. *The Birth of Biopolitics: Lectures at the Collège de France, 1978–1979*. Picador, 2010.

Frank, Thomas, and Matt Weiland. *Commodify Your Dissent: Salvos from the Baffler*. W. W. Norton and Co., 1997.

Franzen, Jonathan. "I'll Be Doing More of the Same." *Review of Contemporary Fiction*, Spring 1996.

Freeman, Jo. "The Tyranny of Structurelessness." *The Second Wave*, 1972.

Frye, Northrop. *Anatomy of Criticism*. Princeton UP, 1957.

Fukuyama, Francis. "The End of History?" *National Interest*, no. 16, Summer 1989.

Gladstone, Brooke. *The Trouble with Reality: A Rumination on Moral Panic in Our Time*. Workman Publishing Co., 2017.

Golding, Alan. "Avant-Gardism against Itself: 'Conversation' and the Reader Critic in the *Little Review*." Lecture delivered at the Pennsylvania State University Department of Comparative Literature, 2 October 2017.

Goodyear, Dana. "The Moneyed Muse." *New Yorker*, 19 February 2007.

Grasshoff, Alexander. *The Wave*. ABC Broadcasting Company, 4 October 1981.

Gray, John. *Liberalism*. U of Minnesota P, 1986.

Greenberg, Clement. "Avant-Garde and Kitsch." *Art and Culture: Critical Essays*. Beacon P, 1961.

Greif, Mark. "What Was the Hipster?" *New York* magazine, 22 October 2010.

Groys, Boris. *The Total Art of Stalinism: Avant-Garde, Aesthetic Dictatorship, and Beyond*. Translated by Charles Rougle. Princeton UP, 1992.

Gutmann, Amy, and Dennis Thompson. *The Spirit of Compromise: Why Governing Demands It and Campaigning Undermines It*. Princeton UP, 2014.

Haddow, Douglas. "Hipster: The Dead End of Western Civilization." *Adbusters* #79, August 2008.

Hanna, Kathleen. Notebook, "Riot Grrrl Test Patterns," undated; Kathleen Hanna Papers; Box 2; Folder 22; Fales Library and Special Collections, New York University Libraries.

Harris, Malcolm. *Kids These Days: Human Capital and the Making of Millennials*. Back Bay Books, 2017.

Hartman, Saidiya. *Scenes of Subjection: Terror, Slavery, and Self-Making in Nineteenth-Century America*. Oxford UP, 1997.

Harvey, David. *A Brief History of Neoliberalism*. Oxford UP, 2005.

Hayes, Terrance. *American Sonnets for My Past and Future Assassin*. Penguin Books, 2018.

Hecht, Ben. *A Child of the Century.* Simon and Schuster, 1950.

Hong, Cathy Park. "Delusions of Whiteness in the Avant-Garde." *Lana Turner*, no. 7, 2014.

Hungerford, Amy. "On Not Reading." *Chronicle of Higher Education*, 11 September 2016.

———. *Making Literature Now.* Stanford UP, 2016.

Hurston, Zora Neale. "How It Feels to Be Colored Me." *The World Tomorrow*, May 1928.

Jefferson, Thomas. "To John Holmes," April 22, 1820, in Paul Leicester Ford, ed., *The Works of Thomas Jefferson*, vol. 10. G. P. Putnam's Sons, 1904.

Kahn, Ashley. "Miles Davis and Bill Evans: Miles and Bill in Black and White." *Jazz Times*, 25 April 2019.

Kakutani, Michiko. "A Country Dying of Laughter. In 1,079 Pages." *New York Times*, 12 February 1996.

Kaplan, Fred. "Kind of Blue." *Slate*, 17 August 2009.

Kavanaugh Hearing: Transcript. *Washington Post.* 27 September 2018.

Kiefer, Brittaney. "Meet the Directors behind New Music Videos for Elton John Classics." *Campaign*, 14 June 2017.

Knausgaard, Karl Ove. *My Struggle*, Book 6. Translated by Don Bartlett and Martin Aitken. Archipelago Books, 2018.

Kocher, Ruth Ellen. "Roundtable on *Citizen: An American Lyric.*" *Los Angeles Review of Books*, 15 December 2014.

Konstantinou, Lee. *Cool Characters: Irony and American Fiction.* Harvard UP, 2016.

Lerner, Ben. *10:04.* Faber and Faber, 2014.

———. *Leaving the Atocha Station.* Coffee House P, 2011.

Levine, Caroline. *Forms: Whole, Rhythm, Hierarchy, Network.* Princeton UP, 2015.

Locke, John. *Second Treatise on Government.* Project Gutenberg, 2010.

Lordi, Emily J. "Beyoncé's Other Women: Considering the Soul Muses of 'Lemonade.'" *Fader*, 6 March 2016.

Losurdo, Domenico. *Liberalism: A Counter-History.* Verso, 2011.

Lyon, Janet. *Manifestoes: Provocations of the Modern*. Cornell UP, 1999.

Marcus, Sara. *Girls to the Front: The True Story of the Riot Grrrl Revolution*. Harper Perennial, 2010.

Margalit, Avishai. *On Compromise and Rotten Compromises*. Princeton UP, 2009.

Martin, Theodore. "The Dialectics of Damage: Art, Form, Formlessness." Nonsite.org, 9 October 2015.

Marx, Karl. "On the Jewish Question." *The Marx-Engels Reader*, ed. Robert Tucker. W. W. Norton and Co., 1978.

Masad, Ilana. "'But I prefer to answer zero questions about it': An Interview with Terrance Hayes." *Prairie Schooner*, 30 March 2018.

McGurl, Mark. *The Program Era: Postwar Fiction and the Rise of Creative Writing*. Harvard UP, 2009.

McInnes, Gavin. "The Right Needs a Dose of Punk Rock Unity." Rebel News, 6 January 2017.

Mesle, Sarah, and Phillip Maciak. "Super Yoncé." *Los Angeles Review of Books*, 8 February 2016.

Monroe, Harriet. "The Open Door." *Poetry: A Magazine of Verse*, November 1912.

Mouffe, Chantal. *Agonistics: Thinking the World Politically*. Verso, 2013.
———. *The Democratic Paradox*. Verso, 2005.

Nelson, Maggie. *The Art of Cruelty: A Reckoning*. W. W. Norton and Co., 2011.

Nguyen, Mimi Thi. "Riot Grrrl, Race, and Revival." *Women & Performance: A Journal of Feminist Theory*, vol. 22, issue 2–3, 2012.

Nietzsche, Friedrich. *On the Genealogy of Morals and Ecce Homo*. Translated by Walter Kaufmann. Vintage Books, 1989.

Nussbaum, Martha. *Poetic Justice: The Literary Imagination of Public Life*. Beacon P, 1997.

"'Orange' Creator Jenji Kohan: 'Piper Was My Trojan Horse.'" *Fresh Air*, NPR, 13 August 2013.

Paige, D. D., ed. *The Selected Letters of Ezra Pound, 1907–1941*. New Directions, 1971.

Poggioli, Renato. *The Theory of the Avant-Garde*. Harvard UP, 1968.

"Political Polarization, Political Compromise and Divisive Policy De-
     bates." U.S. Politics and Policy. Pew Research Center for the People
     and the Press, 18 September 2014.

Rancière, Jacques. *Hatred of Democracy*. Verso, 2014.

Rand, Ayn. *For the New Intellectual*. Penguin Books, 1963.

Rankine, Claudia. *Citizen: An American Lyric*. Graywolf P, 2014.

Reed, Anthony. "The Erotics of Mourning in Recent Experimental Black
     Poetry." *Black Scholar*, vol. 47, 2017.

Rushkoff, Douglas. *Generation Like*. Frontline, PBS, 2014.

Schmitt, Carl. *The Concept of the Political*. Originally published 1932.
     Translated by George Schwab. U of Chicago P, 2007.

Shockley, Evie. "Race, Reception, and Claudia Rankine's 'American
     Lyric.'" *Los Angeles Review of Books*, 6 January 2016.

Shotwell, Alexis. *Against Purity: Living Ethically in Compromised Times*.
     U of Minnesota P, 2016.

Sontag, Susan. "Fascinating Fascism." *New York Review of Books*, 6 Feb-
     ruary 1975.

Spahr, Juliana. *Du Bois's Telegram: Literary Resistance and State Confine-
     ment*. Harvard UP, 2018.

Spice, Anton. "An Introduction to the Electric Sound of Miles Davis."
     VF, 26 April 2016.

"Start a Fucking Riot" Flyer, date unknown; Mark Anderson and
     Positive Force D.C. Riot Grrrl Collection; MSS 445; uncata-
     logued carton #3; Fales Library and Special Collections, New York
     University Libraries.

Strong, Tracy B. "Foreword: Dimensions of the New Debate around
     Carl Schmitt." *The Concept of the Political*, U of Chicago P, 2007.

Swensen, Cole, and David St. John, eds. *American Hybrid: A Norton
     Anthology of New Poetry*. W. W. Norton and Co., 2009.

Szalay, Michael. "The Incorporation Artist." *Los Angeles Review of Books*,
     10 July 2012.

Tamayo, Jennifer. "The Gold Star Awards . . . A message from The
     Mongrel Coalition Against Gringpo." *Harriet*, 2 April 2015.

Trilling, Lionel. *The Liberal Imagination: Essays on Literature and Society*.
     Viking, 1950.

Vail, Tobi. Untitled Essay. *Bikini Kill*, no. 2, circa 1991; Kathleen Hanna Papers; Box 1; Folder 12; Fales Library and Special Collections, New York University Libraries.

Wallace, David Foster. "E Unibus Pluram." *Review of Contemporary Fiction*, vol. 13, no. 2, 1993.

———. Interview with Charlie Rose. *The Charlie Rose Show*, 27 March 1997.

———. "Quo Vadis—Introduction." *Review of Contemporary Fiction*, vol. 16, no. 1, 1996.

Williams, Jeffrey J. "Shakespeare and Scooby-Doo: An Interview with Terrance Hayes." *Iowa Review*, Spring 2018.

Williams, Phillip B. "Letter of Apology from a Ruth Lilly Fellow." Published on Google Docs, 7 June 2020.

Wolff, Rebecca. "Fence Manifesto of 1997." *Jacket 2*, July 2000.

Wood, James, and Karl Ove Knausgaard. "Writing *My Struggle*: An Exchange." *Paris Review*, Winter 2014.

Yu, Timothy. *Race and the Avant-Garde: Experimental and Asian American Poetry since 1965*. Stanford UP, 2009.

IMAGE AND TEXT CREDITS

Page vii: Sleater-Kinney, "The Center Won't Hold." All best efforts have been made to secure permission to reprint these lyrics.

Page 27: Guns N' Roses, "Welcome to the Jungle." All best efforts have been made to secure permission to reprint these lyrics.

Page 45: Elton John, "Tiny Dancer." All best efforts have been made to secure permission to reprint these lyrics.

Page 93: Beyoncé, "Formation." All best efforts have been made to secure permission to reprint these lyrics.

Page 94: Harry How, Pepsi Super Bowl 50 Halftime Show, Getty Images

Page 98: Beyoncé, "Flawless." All best efforts have been made to secure permission to reprint these lyrics.

Page 101: Excerpt from "American Sonnet for My Past and Future Assassin from *American Sonnets for My Past and Future Assassin* by Terrance Hayes, copyright © 2018 by Terrance Hayes. Used by permission of Penguin Books, an imprint of Penguin Publishing Group, a division of Penguin Random House LLC. All rights reserved.

Page 102: Image reproduced with the permission of Terrance Hayes.

Page 108: Glenn Ligon. Untitled: Four Etchings (1992). © Glenn Ligon. Courtesy of the artist, Hauser & Wirth, New York, Regen Projects, Los Angeles, Thomas Dane, London, and Chantal Crousel, Paris.

Page 109: Malevich, Kazimir. *Black Square* (1913–5). Owned by Tretyakov Gallery, Moscow. Oil on linen. Black, textured square on off-white background.

RACHEL GREENWALD SMITH is the author of *Affect and American Literature in the Age of Neoliberalism* (Cambridge University Press, 2015) and editor of two anthologies of scholarship on contemporary literature: *American Literature in Transition: 2000–2010* (Cambridge University Press, 2017) and, with Mitchum Huehls, *Neoliberalism and Contemporary Literary Culture* (Johns Hopkins University Press, 2017). Her essays on contemporary literature, popular culture, and politics have appeared in the *Los Angeles Review of Books*, *Mediations*, *American Literature*, *Novel: A Forum on Fiction*, and elsewhere. She is currently associate professor of English at Saint Louis University.

The text of *On Compromise: Art, Politics, and the Fate of an American Ideal* is set in Whitman. Book design by Rachel Holscher. Composition by Bookmobile Design and Digital Publisher Services, Minneapolis, Minnesota. Manufactured by Versa Press on acid-free, 30 percent postconsumer wastepaper.